Getting into
The Formula of Concord

# Getting into The Formula of Concord

A HISTORY AND DIGEST
OF THE FORMULA

Historical Notes
and Discussion Questions
by
Eugene F. Klug

Translation of the Epitome
by
Otto F. Stahlke

Publishing House
St. Louis

To the people of The Lutheran Church—Missouri Synod
who in their concern for concord strive to remain united
according to the intention and meaning
of the Lutheran Confessions.

Concordia Publishing House, St. Louis, Missouri
Copyright © 1977 Concordia Publishing House
MANUFACTURED IN THE UNITED STATES OF AMERICA

---

Library of Congress Cataloging in Publication Data

Klug, Eugene F
    Getting into the Formula of concord.

    1. Lutheran Church. Formula of concord. I. Stahlke, Otto F., joint author. II. Title.
BX8069.4.K58         238'.4'1         76-28382
ISBN 978-0-7586-4181-6

---

# PREFACE

"Mayday" (from the French *m'aider*, "Help me!") is an international radiotelephone distress signal or call used when life and safety hang in the balance.

The homonym "May Day" refers to May 1, especially as observed with festivals. Another important day in May—the 30th—has for years been our nation's Memorial Day honoring our battlefield dead. Christians, particularly Lutheran Christians, ought to remember still another day in May, the 29th. Four hundred years ago on that date, 1577, six men signed the Formula of Concord, which was destined to become one of history's most important religious documents.

For 30 years after Luther's death terrible dissension and doctrinal unrest tore the Lutheran churches. Things were so bad that a theological Mayday distress call might well have been sounded. The Formula of Concord was God's answer to the people's prayer for help. No compromise document, the Formula was more like a sharp threshing instrument that sifted cleanly between the subtleties of error and the truth of God's Word, establishing God-pleasing unity and concord on the solid base of Holy Scripture.

It is unlikely that the Lutheran Church could have survived without the Formula, at least as a church loyal to the Augsburg Confession.

Do Lutherans today still want to be Lutheran Christians according to the intent and meaning of their Confessions? The importance of this question is seen in the doctrinal distress and dissension that again tear at the church's innards. In our day the Formula of Concord still has answers that serve the cause of unity and concord.

Our present study is based on the Epitome, the shorter, popular version of the Formula, completed at the same time in 1577 and intended for popular use and study. Prof. Otto Stahlke offers a fresh translation for today's readers.

The book's arrangement, with its appended set of

questions, beckons not only the individual reader but especially also discussion groups. Originally the plan was to include outlines of each chapter based on the historical notes. Economy dictated shortening. Each discussion group, however, might still find it helpful to do its own outlining of the historical introductions and the Epitome itself.

This book is the first of a series scheduled to appear by 1980, the 400th anniversary of the Book of Concord, which includes both parts of the Formula of Concord and the other Confessions recognized by the Lutheran Church.

The passing of 400 years has not dimmed the pertinence and viability of what our Lutheran forebears contended for in 1577. God's blessing will undoubtedly attend such study.

Eugene F. Klug

# CONTENTS

General Introduction     9

Events Leading to the Formula of Concord     16

    I. Original Sin     24
       Historical Background:
       The Flacian Controversy

    II. Free Will     29
       Historical Background:
       The Synergistic Controversy

    III. Righteousness of Faith Before God     34
       Historical Background:
       The Osiandrian and Stancarian Controversies

    IV. Of Good Works     38
       Historical Background:
       The Majoristic Controversy

    V. Of the Law and the Gospel     42
       Historical Background:
       The Antinomistic Controversy

    VI. Of the Third Use of the Law     46
       Historical Background:
       The Antinomistic Controversy

    VII. Of the Lord's Supper
         and
    VIII. Of the Person of Christ     49
       Historical Background:
       Crypto-Calvinistic Controversy

    IX. Of the Descent of Christ to Hell     56
       Historical Background:
       Controversy on Christ's Descent into Hell

X. Of Church Rites 59
    Which Are Commonly Called
    Adiaphora or Matters of Indifference

    Historical Background:
    The Adiaphoristic Controversy

XI. Of God's Eternal Foreknowledge and Election 65
    Historical Background:
    A Disputed Subject in Christendom

XII. Of Other Heresies and Sects 70
    Historical Background: Sectarian Movements
    that Had Never Embraced the Augsburg Confession

The Formula of Concord
Part One: The Epitome 75

Questions 108

# General Introduction

Martin Luther's death from natural causes is one of history's miracles. Ever since the Diet of Worms (1521), he lived with a price on his head under the imperial edict of condemnation.

Luther was on one of his many goodwill missions—settling a family dispute between the Princes of Mansfeld—when he died at Eisleben, his birthplace, on Feb. 18, 1546. Seldom, if ever, would Europe's masses mourn a man more deeply. Philipp Melanchthon, Luther's valued colleague on the Wittenberg faculty, announced his death to the students the next day with these words:

> Alas, gone is the horseman and the chariot of Israel! It was he who guided the church in the recent era of the world. It was not human brilliance that discovered the doctrine of the forgiveness of sin and of faith in the son of God, but God who raised him up before our very eyes, who has revealed these truths through him. Let us then hold dear the memory of this man and the doctrine in the very manner in which he delivered it to us. Let us then live more virtuously and remain alert to the grievous afflictions which are bound to follow in the wake of this loss. I beseech you, Son of God, O Immanuel, crucified and risen for us, to save, preserve, and protect your church! (Quoted in O. Thulin, *A Life of Luther,* Philadelphia, 1966, p. 129.)

Melanchthon could not have spoken truer or more eloquent words! Prophetic, too, because tears were not the only thing triggered by Luther's passing. Political and theological strife commenced almost immediately. Pope Paul III and Emperor Charles V resumed their pressure on the Lutheran territories, cities, and princes. This led to the Smalcald War. Disturbances and rival opinions surfaced among Lutherans, threatening to tear the church apart.

For years Luther had been conscious of the force, or power, that centered in his person. It is a tribute to his greatness that he never tried to exploit it. Whatever influence he wielded—and it was great—was always directed for the sake of the Gospel to the good of Christ's church on earth. As a student of history and master of Scripture he sensed the time-bound nature of the Gospel's continuance in its purity at any one place. He foresaw many problems that would arise after his death. Yet he never doubted God's power to enable the church to go on without him. Just a year after the 1530 Diet of Augsburg, high-water mark of the Reformation, Luther said in a sermon on John 7:33-34:

> The Gospel has its day and takes its course from one city to another. Today it is here; tomorrow, there. It is like a heavy shower which passes from place to place . . . . Even if a certain place accepts the Gospel today, it will not stay there long. People hate it; they view it with envy; they curse it; yes, they starve it out. . . . See to it that you do not neglect it; do not sleep your opportunity away. . . . We should not suppose that the Gospel, which we now have, will stay with us forever. Wait, and see what the situation will be in twenty years. Then tell me about it again. After the death of the present pious and sincere pastors, others will appear who will preach and act according to the pleasure of the devil (*Luther's Works*, 23, 261—262).

In his typically down-to-earth manner, Luther illustrated his point further in a way that his Wittenberg audience could not miss:

> The people become weary of the Word and suppose that it will endure forever. When a good beer is available at a certain place, everybody runs there without delay, knowing that the supply will not last long. . . . Therefore people get it while it is to be had. If it could be obtained for a long period of time, our appetite would become surfeited, and the beer would not be prized. But here we assume that the Word will remain with us always, although, in fact, it stays and endures but a short time before it is gone. If you do not accept it gratefully and reverently, you will soon be without it. And once the Word is gone . . . all will prove futile (*Ibid.*, 262—263).

In two of his greatest exegetical works, his *scholia* (lectures) on Galatians (1531) and on Genesis (completed late in 1545), Luther often voiced concern that people would turn away from the purity of God's truth in His holy Word. The *Rottengeister*, that is, factious spirits, as Luther called the fanatics or fantastical sects, were a special worry because of their uncontrolled subjectivism. Even among his colleagues on the Wittenberg faculty Luther noted a compromise spirit on a doctrine as vital as the Lord's Supper, and he fully intended to do something about it when he returned from Eisleben. But God intervened.

Events moved quickly against the Lutherans and their Smalcald League. On June 26, 1546, the pope and emperor drew up a pact, pooling resources and troops to bring the Lutherans to their knees and back to the fold of Rome. A papal bull issued on July 4, 1546, was a virtual crusade call to arms. The sides were not evenly matched. The Smalcald War was over almost before it started. In the initial battle at Muehlberg, April 24, 1547, the Spanish troops and Italian levies crushed Elector John Frederick of Saxony and his forces. The elector was taken captive. With their foremost leader gone, the rest of the Smalcald League was doomed. Territory after territory and city after city fell before the superior forces of the Catholic coalition. Wittenberg, too, bowed to Charles V's troops, but the emperor kept his victorious troops from disturbing Luther's burial place in the Castle Church. Southern and central Germany lay defeated. Much of northern Germany faced the same fate. Adding to the ignominy of defeat was the traitorous role of Duke Moritz of Saxony, nephew of the elector. In return for allying himself and his troops with the Catholic forces he gained the title of Elector of Saxony. Fear was everywhere. People could not believe the sudden turn of events.

On May 15, 1548, the Augsburg Interim was proclaimed by the emperor. Its provisions were a sharp repudiation of the Lutheran position:

> The Council of Trent's decisions on doctrine, once its sessions were concluded, were to be accepted as final;
> Romanist rites and ceremonies were to be reinstated;
> Papal primacy and the authority of the bishops were to be acknowledged;
> All doctrines were to be understood in the Romanist sense, including the seven sacraments and the teaching of transubstantiation in the mass;
> The Reformation's chief article, on justification by faith alone, was virtually canceled out;
> Only two concessions were temporarily allowed: marriage of the Lutheran clergy and the reception of "two kinds" (bread and wine) in the Lord's Supper.

Particularly galling in this whole affair was the part played by Johann Agricola in drawing up these provisions. He had been one of Luther's earliest supporters and friends. At one time, before Luther himself finally took the task in hand, Agricola had even been suggested as the one who should author the Lutheran catechism. The Augsburg Interim stirred immediate resistance and defiance among loyal Lutherans. Swift, severe reprisal came from the emperor's side, especially against the Lutheran pastors. Many were imprisoned; some were killed; most managed to escape out of south Germany to safer regions in the north. Magdeburg replaced Wittenberg as the Lutheran rallying center. John Frederick, a pillar and symbol of strength, never flinched, in spite of the pressures and dishonor of captivity. Melanchthon, too, at first opposed the Interim vigorously, though Wittenberg itself had fallen. But other princes gave in rather than pay the price of prolonged captivity.

After Luther's death the mantle of theological leadership fell naturally to Melanchthon. But he had never been strong under pressure. With Luther gone, there was no one to lean on, and Melanchthon's theological vacillations now could not be stabilized. He feared for his life; he feared for the future of the Lutheran church; and Moritz seized the opportunity to pressure him into composing a substitute document for the Augsburg Interim, something less distasteful to the Lutheran party. The result was the Leipzig Interim, which was adopted at the Diet in that city on Dec. 22, 1548.

The only positive accomplishment of the Leipzig Interim was the reopening of the University of Wittenberg. In every other way it was a disaster. Melanchthon's idea had been to yield merely on adiaphora, that is, matters neither commanded nor forbidden by Scripture, but in fact his concessions closely paralleled the Augsburg Interim, with the extra onus of being written by Melanchthon, erstwhile right-hand man of Luther. Even the article on justification was missing, and the Roman Catholic works-righteous theology—the Reformation's chief target—was given much elbow room. Thus the Leipzig Interim could only be characterized as a compromised, unionistic document. And the man who had once written the formidable treatise on the Power and Primacy of the Pope (appendix to the Smalcald Articles of Luther, 1537) now reneged meekly on the question of the papacy as the Antichrist. It was a black hour for Lutheran theology and undoubtedly the blunder of Melanchthon's life. Staunch Lutheran theologians castigated him severely for his abject capitulations. Even John Calvin censured him with biting pen, exclaiming that a leader who flinches in battle is many times more reprehensible than a whole troop of soldiers who flee the field.

After Leipzig leadership among the Lutherans was up for grabs. Theologians like Matthias Flacius, Johann Herrmann, Nikolaus von Amsdorf, Kaspar Aquila, and Johann Wigand competed for the post Melanchthon had lost by default. The talented and fiery Flacius, originally from the Balkan region of Illyria, proved at first to be the most eloquent spokesman for loyal Lutheran teaching, and he vigorously opposed Melanchthon, his old colleague on the Wittenberg faculty.

But politics, more than theology, shaped unfolding events. Moritz, popularly known as the "Judas of Meissen" because of his earlier treachery, suddenly switched sides again. He drove the emperor from Innsbruck, sent the Catholic officials, bishops, and fathers scurrying out of Trent, and on Aug. 5, 1552, entered Augsburg in triumph as the "rescuer" of the Lutheran cause. The resulting Treaty, or Convention, of Passau, Aug. 2, 1552, brought an end to the Interims. With the Peace of Augsburg, 1555, Lutherans for the first time gained the right to exist and practice their faith freely.

But by this time the victory was bittersweet, for within the Lutheran church itself there was chaos. Dissension and disunity reigned as a result of the struggle between conservative and moderate factions, between those concerned to keep Lutheran teaching pure and those somewhat indifferent to doctrinal purity and open to compromise. At the eye of the storm stood Melanchthon, ever the vacillating theologian, still a sort of humanist and pious moralist. His shoulders were not ample enough to take up and wear Luther's mantle.

Polarization of theological positions around leaders like Melanchthon and Flacius became intense. Each side claimed heirship to the Augsburg Confession and the other Lutheran Confessions. The "Philippists" (named after Philipp Melanchthon) stood for a moderate, compromise position in doctrine; the "Gnesio-Lutherans" (that is, "genuine Lutherans"—so they claimed to be), following Flacius, stood for absolute loyalty and strict, stern discipline in accord with Lutheran principles.

Under these extremely charged conditions sharp words

and actions drove an ever deeper wedge between the sides and sundered every vestige of Lutheran solidarity. Controversies erupted on multiple questions which were not settled until another group of concerned theological leaders and Lutheran laymen came to the fore, chiefly in the mid-1560s and early 1570s. Men like Martin Chemnitz, Jakob Andreae, Johann Brenz, David Chytraeus, Christoph Koerner, Joachim Moerlin, and Nikolaus Selnecker, with a host of loyal laymen, now appeared as a third group, totally loyal to the position of Luther and of the Lutheran Confessions but also able to pour oil on the troubled waters and resolve the sharp doctrinal differences. The Formula of Concord was their time-honored achievement. After 30 years of strife it brought peace and unity to sorely tried Lutheran theology and to its lands and people throughout Europe.

Following are the controversies that arose after the Interim, with their approximate dates and key issues. The pertinent Formula of Concord articles are noted in parentheses:

1. **Adiaphoristic, 1548—55 (FC X)** Melanchthon: demands of the Leipzig Interim are adiaphora, hence acceptable and not divisive. Flacius and the Formula: Nothing is an adiaphoron in case of confession and offense.

2. **Majoristic, 1551—62 (FC IV)** Georg Major and Justus Menius: good works are necessary to salvation. Amsdorf: good works are detrimental .... The Formula: good works are necessary as fruits of faith, but not "to salvation."

3. **Synergistic, 1555—60 (FC II)** Melanchthon and others: man cooperates in his own conversion. Flacius and the Formula: God alone converts man, though man's person and will are involved. Conversion is God's work; man and his will are purely passive.

4. **Flacian, 1560—75 (FC I)** Direct outgrowth of the Synergistic Controversy. Flacius and others: original sin is a substantive part of man's nature, not accidental. The Formula: original sin is not part of man's substance, and yet it is so deeply infixed that man is totally corrupt by nature.

5. **Osiandristic-Stancarian, 1549—66 (FC III)** Andreas Osiander the Elder denied the forensic sense of justifica-

tion and insisted that we become righteous by Christ's indwelling according to His divine nature. Franciscus Stancarus taught that Christ is our righteousness only according to His human nature. The Formula: Christ is our righteousness according to both natures. Faith is reckoned for righteousness for His sake.

6. **Antinomistic, 1527—56 (FC V and VI)** Agricola had long insisted that repentance is worked alone by the Gospel. Andreas Poach and Anton Otto denied the 3rd use of the Law. The Formula: both Law and Gospel, properly distinguished according to their respective functions, are necessary; the Law is a rule (3d use) also for Christians.

7. **Crypto-Calvinistic, 1560—74 (FC VII and VIII)** Philippists confounded the doctrine of the Lord's Supper and of the real, substantial presence of Christ's body and blood; also distorted the doctrine on the full communication of divine attributes to Christ according to His human nature. Opposed by theologians like Chemnitz, Brenz, Joachim Westphal, and Tilemann Hesshusius, whose views are reflected in the Formula.

8. **Descent into Hell (FC IX)** Johannes Aepinus, among others, taught that it belonged to Christ's state of humiliation. The Formula: Christ's descent to hell was triumphant and the beginning of his exaltation according to the human nature.

9. **Predestination (FC XI)** Erroneous views concerning a Christian's perseverance in faith, challenged especially by Johannes Marbach of Strasbourg. The Formula: God's divine election is the cause of the believers' salvation; the lost are lost by their own fault.

The 12th article of the Formula of Concord dealt with the sects and their doctrinal aberrations.

# Events Leading to the Formula of Concord

Thirty years of strife, not over territories, but over doctrine, followed Luther's death. Lutherans were divided, a dilemma that brought comfort to their adversaries, both Catholic and Reformed. One main issue in divided Lutheranism concerned the question of what constituted a sufficient basis for unity and fellowship. One side, Melanchthon and the Philippists, stood for a more moderate, compromising position that would allow the churches to remain in union even though not in perfect agreement. The other side, Flacius and the strict Lutherans, demurred completely, labeling this position "unionistic compromise" and "indifferentism." Flacius held that unity in the church could come only with the restoration of genuine peace, with genuine agreement on controverted issues.

For 20 years after Luther's death Lutheran leaders, theologians, and laymen spent themselves in quest of a formula that would heal the division. But despite earnest efforts the split seemed to widen. Theologians and lay leaders, chiefly princes, met 1556 at Weimar to set up conditions for peace. The meeting turned out to be a confrontation and standoff between the sympathizers of Flacius and Melanchthon's supporters. Flacius wanted to establish a firm position against false teachings and heresies that had crept into the church—synergism, Majorism, adiaphorism, Crypto-Calvinism—and he spared no words in accusing Melanchthon as partly responsible for their intrusion. Melanchthon bristled and bridled, with the result that the split became increasingly bitter. But though he finally yielded to Flacius on at least one point, namely his responsibility for the Adiaphoristic controversy, it was a rather hopeless situation. Efforts by other negotiators, including Moerlin and Chemnitz, led nowhere. Animosity mounted as Flacius pressed for complete admission of guilt by the Philippists, and Melanchthon scrambled to protect his sullied reputation.

Efforts from on top, by the princes, also accomplished little. Preparing for an upcoming meeting with the Catholics, the Lutherans met at Frankfurt, June 1557, in an effort to iron out their own differences first—but to no avail. They came to the Sept. 1557 colloquy of Worms quite divided and met mockery at the hands of the Catholic representatives, who had not favored the meeting in the first place. The latter even urged that the conditions of the Peace of Augsburg (1555) be rescinded, since conditions were so bad among the Lutherans. The Jesuits particularly aggravated an already painful situation by claiming that the dissension proved that the Lutherans themselves had departed from their own chief formula, the Augsburg Confession (1530).

The jibing by the adversaries had at least one favorable effect: it prodded the Lutheran princes to expend every effort to find a way out of their embarrassment. But peace with compromise, in line with customary political tactics, was the only route with which they were familiar. The disputed Frankfurt Recess was such a product, an unfortunate offspring of their ill-fated efforts. Flacius quickly spelled out in detail the great wrong of this unionistic compromise that settled no differences. Thereupon Elector August of Saxony enlisted Melanchthon's help in drafting a defense. Flacius promptly dashed off another reply, the Book of Confutation and, with others, pleaded for a general synod of all Lutherans. This plea, a kind of last-ditch effort written by Flacius, was titled "Supplication." But Melanchthon opposed the idea, and because August, his prince, supported him, the whole matter never got off the ground.

In addition to religious peace the princes wanted civil peace. They met 1561 at Naumburg and tried to settle matters without the theologians; but they failed, because they could not agree on whether to stand by the Unaltered Augsburg Confession of 1530 or by the so-called *Variata*, the Augsburg Confession as amended by Melanchthon in 1540. A deeper, more basic reason lay at the root of their difficulties. Some of them, whether they knew or admitted it or not, had gone over to the Calvinistic side on the doctrine of the Lord's Supper. Crypto-Calvinism was the real threat, along with a surrender of Luther's position on the doctrine of the Real Presence of Christ's body and blood in the Sacrament. Could fellowship exist or be established between parties that stood apart on this article of faith?

This was to be the chief hurdle. Meetings, convocations, confrontations, and compromise formulas would not advance the cause of unity one inch until this issue was settled. In fact it was destined to become the key of future Lutheran relations. Unity and fellowship in the faith would come to be seen as grounded on clear, unequivocal agreement in doctrine. Peace in the Lutheran church had to wait until agreement was reached on this important point.

This goal could not be achieved until there were new leaders, other than Melanchthon and Flacius, who could rally Lutherans everywhere to support this position on doctrinal purity. Two stand out in this quest for peace and unity— Andreae and Chemnitz. They helped bind the wounds of dissension-torn Lutheranism with a formula of concord. Andreae hailed from Weiblingen, Wuerttemberg, where he was born in 1528. A student of the loyal Lutheran theologian Brenz, Andreae became professor and chancellor at the University of Tuebingen, Wuerttemberg.

Chemnitz was born Nov. 9, 1522, in Treuenbrietzen, a hamlet that lay midway between Wittenberg and Berlin. He studied at the University of Wittenberg, but in the field of mathematics, not theology. So, though he had opportunity to see and hear Luther preach, especially the year before the Reformer died, he never benefited directly by attending his classroom lectures. Chemnitz was largely self-taught theologically, achieving his unrivalled theological competence almost entirely during the two- to three-year period when he supervised the ducal library at Koenigsberg. It was a productive time in his life, during which he applied himself assiduously to a study of Scripture in the original languages and to all the writings of Luther. Eventually he put in a short stint of teaching at Wittenberg as Melanchthon's understudy. At that same time he gained his certification as preacher and then left Wittenberg to become coadjutor with Moerlin in the territorial church of Brunswick. Eventually the superintendent's post became his when Moerlin moved to Koenigsberg.

Apparently Chemnitz and Andreae met for the first time at the Sept. 1557 meeting with the Catholic theologians at Worms. But their acquaintance first became really close in 1568, when Duke Julius of Brunswick invited Andreae to help

Chemnitz with the church visitation in his territory. Together they drew up the *Corpus Doctrinae Julium,* which was a kind of confession of faith and a guideline for order and worship in the churches. It was spadework that set the stage for their collaboration on a formula of concord.

The pilot effort at something that could be called a forerunner of the formula came in 1569 when Andreae set forth five topics for consideration and discussion—justification, good works, free will, adiaphora, and the Lord's Supper—and distributed them as a possible formula for concord to various theologians for comment. Response was mixed. Some approved what he had written; others criticized it as incomplete and lacking in sharp antitheses against erroneous doctrinal positions. It led, however, to the invitation of Andreae to Wittenberg (1569) by Elector August for consultation with his theologians at the university. These meetings seemed to come off well. Andreae apparently thought that these erstwhile Philippists were in sympathy with his position.

But later Andreae met in Brunswick with Chemnitz, who pointed out to him that the Wittenbergers, while attesting support for the historic Lutheran position according to the Augsburg Confession, had done so according to the disputed *Corpus Philippicum,* or *Misnicum,* which supported Melanchthon's views. Thus their guarded language had another meaning and intent. That there was a certain deviousness in their theological dealings soon became plain through a catechism issued at Wittenberg; the book had all the earmarks of Calvinism, especially as regards the Lord's Supper. Chemnitz immediately wrote an evaluation of this catechism, circulating a kind of confessional statement throughout the territorial churches of Brunswick. He also enlisted the support of men like Hartmann of Frankfurt, Marbach of Strasbourg, and Andreae of Tuebingen. At the same time in his letters to these leaders he pressed for a common confession of faith which would uphold the Augsburg Confession and refute Crypto-Calvinism.

Andreae, tireless traveler and diplomat for Lutheran unity, issued *Six Sermons* on the controverted issues. But Chemnitz and others felt that the sermonic style was unsuited for the intended purpose; they opted for a form which included thesis and antithesis in clearcut, unambiguous statement of fact, article for article. Accordingly, Andreae drafted what was known as the *Swabian Concordia* in eleven articles. This was in essence the first draft of what became the Solid, or Thorough, Declaration of the Formula of Concord. It was again submitted to the Lower Saxony theologians and freely revised, especially by Chemnitz on the article on Free Will and by Chytraeus on the doctrine of the Lord's Supper. In its revised form, as a result of which it became known as the *Swabian-Saxon Concordia,* it was returned to the Swabian theologians for their opinion. By now the time was Sept. 1575. Their criticism focused on the somewhat heavy style, the Latin phrases, and the fact that Melanchthon rather than Luther was so frequently quoted.

Meanwhile Elector August had finally (1574) come to understand and see through the deviousness of his theologians at Wittenberg on the doctrine of the Lord's Supper. Now he knew that these men had been speaking with forked tongues, using Lutheran-sounding terms, but freighting them with Reformed or Calvinistic meaning. Duly alarmed by the Crypto-Calvinistic inroad into his territory, the elector entrusted Lucas Osiander the Elder and Balthasar Bidembach with the task of writing an uncomplicated rebuttal of the errors that threatened Lutheran theology. He wanted them to avoid Latin and technical terminology, as well as quotations from Melanchthon—whose influence was now more and more being recognized as a chief contributing factor to the confusion in Lutheran theology—and to omit reference to sects like the Anabaptists and Schwenkfelders who were no longer a threat to the Lutheran church. In all it had nine articles. It was published in 1575, taking the name *Maulbronn Formula* from the name of the place where the convocation of theologians had taken place.

Now there were two documents addressing the issues. Elector August submitted both of them to Andreae for an opinion. Even though he had had a hand in the *Swabian-Saxon Concordia,* Andreae, acting very objectively, indicated that he favored the *Maulbronn Formula* for reason of style and form. Moreover, he suggested to the elector that a general conference of selected theologians be assembled for critical evaluation of the two documents.

Selnecker headed the 12 theologians who had been invited to Castle Lichtenburg, near Prettin on the Elbe, Feb. 15—17, 1576. Selnecker, who before the unmasking of the Crypto-Calvinists at Wittenberg had himself been ambivalent on the doctrine of the Lord's Supper, was now a convinced and loyal

Lutheran. It was the suggestion of this conclave that past hard feelings be forgiven, that citations from Melanchthon's writings be avoided, and that a broader group, including Chemnitz and Chytraeus from North Germany, be invited to a convocation that would have as its purpose the formulation of a document that could serve as an instrument for concord and unity. Elector August, along with other like-minded lay leaders, sponsored and convened a meeting of 20 theologians at Castle Hartenfeld, Torgau, from May 28 to June 7, 1576.

With painstaking care these men pored over the two existing formulas, *Maulbronn* and *Swabian-Saxon,* and worked out a careful distillation that combined what was best in each of them into a new document. It became known as the "Torgau Book" and included the 12 articles of the later Formula of Concord. In every respect it was a happy meeting, with all the participants rejoicing over the consensus that prevailed on each of the articles, most of which had been sorely disputed during the past 30 years. All were grateful to God for the progress that had been made. It was like a dream come true, Chemnitz felt. When the document was finally delivered to Elector August on June 7, he received it gratefully as an answer to his fervent prayers, and before the theologians departed to their homes he asked Selnecker to conduct a service of thanksgiving.

Copies of the "Torgau Book" were sent out in all directions, to princes, estates, cities, and their clergy and theologians for criticism and evaluation. The speed and reception rivaled that of Luther's 95 Theses. Most comments were favorable, though resistance against a new confession was strong on the part of some, especially among the pro-Calvinistic sections of Europe. Assurance was given, however, that this was not to be a new confession in the usual sense but was merely to state what in fact it meant to be a Lutheran Christian according to the meaning and intent of the Augsburg Confession. Some advised—a suggestion not adopted—that errorists like Flacius, Osiander, Major, and Melanchthon be named in the document along with their faulty notions. Still another suggestion, which gained immediate favor, was that a shorter version also be published simultaneously. In all the Elector received 25 *Gutachten,* or opinions. These he handed over to a select committee of three men, Chemnitz, Andreae, and Selnecker, for careful review. This "triumvirate of the Formula of Concord" met at Cloister Bergen, near

Magdeburg, beginning March 1, 1577, and carefully examined the whole document, considering the various suggestions. Later, in May, they were joined by Chytraeus, Koerner, and Andreas Musculus, and again they went through the whole document with painstaking attention to every detail, revising as necessary or desirable.

Finally on May 28, 1577, the committee of 6 completed their work, which by now had come to be known as the "Bergic Book." This is the part of the Formula of Concord known as the Solid, or Thorough, Declaration. A shorter version, the Epitome, written by Andreae, was also submitted for scrutiny and adoption by that same date. On May 29, 1577, the 6 men affixed their signatures in happy consensus and relief over an arduous task complete at last. Later a Preface, an important declaration of Scriptural position, was added to obviate a number of misunderstandings and to express a platform to which others, particularly the leading lay figures, like the princes, were affixing their signatures. In the course of time the name Formula of Concord came to apply in a narrow sense to the "Bergic Book," which served as a basis for peace, and in a wider sense, as in the *Book of Concord,* to the combination of the Epitome and the "Bergic Book." (For brevity's sake the Epitome is the basis of study in this book.)

When the 6 theologians set their signatures to the Formula of Concord and the Epitome, they did so with the following solemn words:

> Since now, in the sight of God and of all Christendom, we wish to testify to those now living and those who shall come after us that this declaration herewith presented concerning all the controverted articles aforementioned and explained, and no other, is our faith, doctrine, and confession, in which we are also willing, by God's grace, to appear with intrepid hearts before the judgment-seat of Jesus Christ, and give an account of it; and that we will neither privately nor publicly speak or write anything contrary to it, but, by the help of God's grace, intend to abide thereby: therefore, after mature deliberation, we have, in God's fear and with the invocation of His name, attached our signatures with our own hands.

Their work was now sent throughout Europe, into all territories and cities where the Lutheran Reformation had penetrated. The calling of a general synod was held to be inadvisable. Instead, each territory and each individual was to study the documents carefully, with deliberative attention and hopefully with acceptance and subscription. Those who objected on principle to any proposal of a new confession were assured that the Formula of Concord was not a new confession and introduced no new articles but was rather an exposition and defense of the Lutheran Confessions commonly held at this time; it was to serve as a standard against various errors that had crept in after Luther's death, particularly through Romanism, Calvinism, indifferentism, synergism, unionism, and the spirit of compromise. Thus the Formula of Concord and the Epitome, without compromise, asserted the true, pure position on Scripture's teaching in accord with the Confessions previously subscribed. Scripture was still the sole authority, the absolute norm which governed and stood above all other authority, including the Confessions.

Seldom, if ever, had the articles of faith, at least those which had been under such severe testing and controversy, been set forth so clearly and with such careful attestation from the Scriptures. Thus it could be claimed that the Formula and the Epitome were genuinely ecumenical documents. They provided a genuine basis for unity and fellowship, if such was ever to be attained among the splintered groups in Christendom, especially between the Lutheran and Reformed churches.

Subscription to the Formula and the Epitome came spontaneously and freely from all quarters of Lutheranism. While opposition and criticism welled up from Lutheran theology's opponents, the fact remains that no instrument has served so well to guard the articles of faith. This was not merely the work of 6 men. It was the fruit of God's working effectively through His Word in His church, calling His people to faithful and loyal affirmation of His teachings. Charles Porterfield Krauth, along with C. F. W. Walther among the leading Lutheran theologians in America, has put the Formula's significance to the world thus:

> But for the Formula of Concord it may be questioned whether Protestantism could have been saved to the world. It staunched the wounds at which Lutheranism was bleeding to death; and crises were at hand in history in which Lutheranism was essential to the salvation of the Reformatory interest in Europe. The Thirty Years' War, the war of martyrs, which saved our modern world, lay indeed in the future of another century, yet it was fought and settled in the

Cloister at Bergen. But for the pen of the peaceful triumvirate, the sword of Gustavus had not been drawn. Intestine treachery and division in the Church of the Reformation would have done what the arts and arms of Rome failed to do. But the miracle of restoration was wrought. From being the most distracted Church on earth, the Lutheran Church had become the most stable. The blossom put forth at Augsburg, despite the storm, the mildew, and the worm, had ripened into the full round fruit of the amplest and clearest Confession in which the Christian Church has ever embodied her faith. (Quoted in *Concordia Triglotta*, CPH, St. Louis, 1921, Hist. Intr., p. 254.)

# I. Original Sin

## Historical Background:
## THE FLACIAN CONTROVERSY

This was an unfortunate controversy. Not only did it trouble the Lutheran church on an issue that had been settled earlier, but it also marked the downfall of one of the Lutheran church's ablest, most ardent defenders, Matthias Flacius. In 1877, in *Der Concordienformel Kern und Stern,* the book which Dr. C. F. W. Walther issued in commemoration of the 300th anniversary of the Formula of Concord, Missouri's esteemed founder said of Flacius:

> It was a great pity that Flacius, who had hitherto been such a faithful champion of the pure doctrine, exposed himself to the enemies in such a manner. Henceforth the errorists were accustomed to brand all those as Flacianists who were zealous in defending the pure doctrine of Luther. (Quoted in *Concordia Triglotta,* Hist. Int., p. 144.)

Neither Walther nor concerned conservative theologians in our day are rightly called Flacianists. Flacius' zeal for genuine Lutheran theology they share, yes; but his error in connection with original sin, no!

In order to understand how this controversy started, one must see it as closely intertwined with the Synergistic Controversy, which is covered under the second article of the Formula of Concord. At issue was the question: Did man, or did he not, cooperate in his conversion? Like Luther, Flacius stated that fallen man has no powers of his own by which to begin, assist, or sustain his conversion in any way, even in the slightest. The converted sinner owes his faith and the change brought about in him entirely to the Holy Spirit's gracious working in him through the Word.

This Flacius knew, and this he taught clearly. However, with him on the University of Jena faculty was Victorinus Strigel, a Philippist and a synergist. As a defender of

Melanchthon, Strigel was not above embarrassing Flacius if he could find his Achilles' heel. His opportunity came 1560 in the Colloquium at Weimar. This conference's subject was to be conversion and the capacity of the human will. Strigel carefully veiled his synergistic view that man assists in his conversion, shifted the focus on original sin, and caught Flacius off guard with this question: After man's fall is original sin actually a part of man's very substance, or should it be thought of as accidental to his nature? Flacius, instead of sticking to the subject, which was conversion, and the part which the human will played in it, let his opponent put words in his mouth and answered that "after the Fall original sin is not merely accidental to man's nature but in fact the very substance of man."

Flacius no doubt wanted merely to stress the deep depravity and corruption affecting human nature after the Fall, how impossible it is for the human will to act positively in spiritual matters by its native powers. His close friends and colleagues Wigand and Musaeus urged him to restate his position. He ought not simply identify original sin with the substance or nature of man, they cautioned. To say that, would mean that man's body and soul were evil in their very substance. That could imply that God, as creator, was responsible for such a condition in fallen man. The alternative, that Satan was the creator of this evil "substance" in man, was equally bad. That would have resurrected the old dualistic error of Manichaeism, a syncretistic philosophy/theology that envisioned two antagonistic powers, the Power of Light and the Power of Darkness, as competing creative forces in the world. It had been rejected by the early Christian church specifically in the words of the first article of the Nicene Creed, "I believe in one God, the Father Almighty, Maker of heaven and earth, and of *all* things visible and invisible."

Flacius, learned theologian that he was, completely repudiated the Manichaean heresy. But he refused to back off his statement that original sin was the very substance of man. Strigel, however, had boxed him in by getting him to disavow that original sin was an "accident" or something merely accidental to man's nature. Flacius feared that this would imply that the human will after the Fall would still possess basic spiritual powers. The fact is that Scripture and Luther stress the deep depravity resulting from man's fall, yet speak of sin as intruding on the nature of man, not as a constitutive part of that nature itself. Scripture taught a parallel truth that explained everything. Even as the image of God in man was lost without essential loss of the human nature—that is, man remained man though not without radical spiritual loss—so, sin could (and did) enter in and drastically affect and change man. Though his essential nature as such, body and soul, would not simply be identifiable with sin, the terrible taint of it could twist body, soul, and mind into sinful paths so utterly that man could not of himself work a change, or conversion, not even begin or assist in it. This is how Flacius should have answered his opponent, stating that original sin was actually "accidental" to, or an intrusion on, man's nature or substance; for while the sinner, body and soul, could be redeemed from sin, sanctified, and resurrected into glory, his sin would now have to be expiated by God's gracious working. Sin indeed had insinuated itself into man's nature through man's fall. But to speak of it as belonging to the essence or substance of man would create the impossible and implausible state of affairs where it, too, would have to be redeemed, sanctified, etc.

Flacius persisted in his hard-nosed position, especially in his use of "substance" in connection with original sin and man's nature. He expressly denied any sympathy for the Manichaean notion, as well as any basic change in man's physical makeup after the fall. But, he cited Scripture verses and quotations from Luther in an effort to justify himself. A large number of followers stood with him. Everyone recognized, of course, that he had been one of Luther's most eloquent defenders. This fact served now to compound the confusion in many minds.

However, a considerable number of theologians saw through the word-battle and persisted in their repudiation of Flacius' stubborn attachment to "original sin as part of the substance of man." At the same time they discerned the wily intent of Strigel who was using Flacius to camouflage his synergistic views. Later Strigel showed his true colors by joining up with the Reformed.

The decade-long dispute finally was resolved through the Formula's first article. Meanwhile Flacius and many of his followers came into disgrace, lost stature and position, and were forced to move unceremoniously from place to place. To the end of his life Flacius persisted that with his view he was being loyal to Luther.

The Formula of Concord bore straight down on the points at issue. It rejected, on the one hand, Strigel's notion that original sin was "accidental" in the sense that it was only an external, slight, insignificant impairment or impediment which merely weakened man's spiritual powers. On the other hand, it also gave a lucid, simple explanation of Flacius's error (without mentioning his name), explained why it had to be rejected, and then cited Luther with obvious intent of dissociating his name from Flacius's strange position. There was need to set the church straight on whether Flacius was quoting or interpreting the Reformer correctly or not. Accordingly, the Formula states:

> Luther calls this original sin "natural, personal, or essential evil," not intending that "man's nature, person, or essence" is itself "original sin" without distinction, but that these words should distinguish between original sin, which has become infixed into man's nature, and the other sins, which are called actual sins. . . . It is man's nature and character to sin and to be sinful. Here the word "nature" does not designate the substance of man, but something which adheres to his nature or substance. . . . The difference between God's work and the devil's is most clearly demonstrated in this way: the devil cannot create substance; he can only by God's permission corrupt the substance created by God in aspects not related to substance" (Epitome, I, 10—13).

Thus while the Formula avoided completely the notion of identifying original sin with man's nature or substance, it underscored heavily the impact which it had on man and his nature ever since the fall.

# II. Free Will

Historical Background:
THE SYNERGISTIC CONTROVERSY

Man has been described as being incurably religious. That fact is borne out by the multiplicity of his gods. Just as true, it seems, is the statement that all men are by nature "born synergists." "Synergism" means "a working together." Human reason argues that if the way back to God is to be found or worked out, it will have to include something of man's own doing.

Christianity has never succeeded in wiping out the synergistic streak even in regenerate man. Although the Bible stresses that man is saved alone by the grace of God, without the works of the law, the trail of Christian history is littered with the remains of synergistic intrusion on God's Gospel and on the lives of people in whom that Gospel has kindled faith and renewal.

One of the most important things Luther ever wrote was *On the Bondage of the Will* (1525). Erasmus had attacked Luther's position on free will in order to try to redeem himself in the eyes of his Romanist patrons. While regretting Erasmus's action, Luther thanked him for zeroing in on the crucial issue, or "hinge on which our discussion turns," namely, "to investigate what ability 'free-will' has, in what respect it is the subject of divine action and how it stands related to the grace of God," rather than on peripheral matters, like "the papacy, purgatory, indulgences, and such like" (Packer-Johnston eds., *Luther's Bondage of the Will,* Revell, Westwood, N. J., 1957, p. 78). What part did the human will play in conversion? This was the critical question. Was man able of himself to choose the good and leave the evil, and thus be saved? Or when assisted by the infusion of the grace of God? As free decision? Merely as nonresisting will? Or was the will passive in conversion, in the sense that it was to be excluded as a factor that contributed something, anything, at the moment when God's grace alone worked the miracle of regeneration?

Human reason has persistently crossed swords with the teaching of Holy Scripture on this matter. The apostle Paul earnestly poses the alternatives with irrefutable logic in Rom. 11:6; "If by grace, then is it no more of works: otherwise grace is no more grace." This truth, reinforced in many other passages, e.g., Rom. 3:28, Gal. 5:4, Eph. 2:8-9, is simply not palatable to human reason. Reason gets caught in the syndrome of its own dialectic and argues: if man can successfully thwart God's grace by unbelief, then it must be by man's free choice that God's grace is accepted. To human reason there is no alternative, no other way of explaining why some are saved and others lost, than by referral to the human volitional capacity either in assent to or in rejection of God's grace. Otherwise, so runs the argument, one would have to suppose contrary wills in God, according to which He condemns some and saves others.

After the turning point came in Luther's life, he understood and believed with all his heart what the Scriptures taught concerning salvation by grace alone: that Christ's perfect righteousness was imputed unto him freely by grace and received entirely by faith for the forgiveness of sins. From then till the end of his life Luther preached with conviction his "new gospel" which was not new, of course, but everlasting truth of God from the time that the promise was first given after the fall. The *sola gratia/sola fide* ("by grace alone/by faith alone") doctrine was the throbbing heart of the Reformation. Synergism in any form had to be recognized as a return to the Law-oriented theology of Romanism.

As long as Luther was alive he was able to keep the synergistically inclined theologians around him under control. Among them was Melanchthon, one of the most learned lay theologians the church has ever had. He was honored as the *praeceptor Germaniae* ("teacher of Germany"). His contributions affect curriculum planning to this day in the whole educational process.

Melanchthon's earlier theological works were the soundest. The first edition of his dogmatics, *Loci communes,* and his work on the Augsburg Confession (1530) and the Apology (1531) were brilliantly clear on the article on justification by faith alone. But Melanchthon could never completely put down the tendencies of his humanist background. Implicit in this thinking were the inherent capabilities of the human will and its freedom to act. Again and again he posited the nonresisting will of man as a factor in conversion. The later editions of his *Loci,* as well as the *Variata* of 1540, show him stressing man's assenting will as a third cause, besides the Holy Spirit and the Word, in conversion.

Melanchthon's reputation, however, was such that it shielded him for a long time from criticism, though his statements on conversion were increasingly ambiguous. The exposé did not really come until more and more of his students began peddling the synergistic doctrine.

In the first 10 years after Luther's death the distasteful Interims occupied everyone's attention. Finally the Philippists dropped their disguise. It became increasingly evident that the Lutheran church was slipping back into Romanism on the article of justification. If God's grace was needed merely to stimulate and excite the human will and cause it to respond favorably, then theology had come back to the position of the Scholastics and Thomas Aquinas.

Johann Pfeffinger, professor at the University of Leipzig, who had assisted Melanchthon in framing the Leipzig Interim and who was one of his most ardent disciples, openly maintained the significance of the human will's free decision or action in conversion. Man cooperates, he stated, by preparing himself for God's grace and by not resisting when grace comes to him. In 1555 Pfeffinger published his controversial treatise "Five Questions Concerning the Liberty of the Human Will." Now the controversy was out in the open, especially when he cited Melanchthon as his supporting authority. To Pfeffinger's side came Strigel, professor at Jena. By 1559 the controversy was so intense that Duke John Frederick II of Saxony applied the arm of the state and imprisoned some of the protagonists, including Strigel.

These harsh measures were generally deplored, and there was general appeal for an open meeting. This prompted the Weimar disputation (1560), at which Flacius and Strigel became the two leading participants. The topic was to center on free will and the part that the human will played, if any, in the conversion of the sinner. Strigel managed to shift some of the onus from himself and his fellow synergists by successfully leading Flacius into erroneous statements concerning the nature of original sin. (Compare Chapter I above.) Meanwhile he himself used persuasive, rationalistic power to show how the will of man is actively involved in conversion, how it is not spiritually dead, and how, once original sin's power is broken, the natural powers of the will are free to respond and assent on their own.

Luther had taught that man, with his God-given endowment of mind, will, and heart, is indeed a fit subject for conversion. God did not make heaven for geese! But man could not in any way begin, assist, or cooperate in his conversion with his native powers. To know, assent to, and trust in God's grace is something *God* draws forth by the Gospel. The power to resist does not imply power to cooperate. Whereas Strigel believed that there was a remnant of positive, spiritual ability in fallen man that could be stimulated by the grace of God, Luther held that the Scriptures made it plain that man and his will were totally corrupted by original sin, so that man was spiritually worse off than a block of stone or a lifeless corpse. Man's rebirth or regeneration by the grace and power of the Holy Ghost through the Word was, therefore, entirely worked by the power of God. Thus man, as regards his conversion, said Luther, is *mere passive* or completely passive (Weimar ed., 18, 697).

Luther did not doubt that the human will was involved, that the mind was enlightened, that the trust of man was evoked in man's conversion; but all such change affecting mind, will, and heart was to be traced to God's grace working in him. If this were not so, then salvation would not in fact be by grace alone, but in part by human effort or cooperation. God's grace converts; it does not merely incite or begin a process that man completes. Luther never doubted that, once man is converted, the will, as also the mind and heart, moved with new life. But even then, in the renewal of life, sanctification or good works, the source of enabling power still lay in God's grace working in the believer.

The controversy raged on in the 1560s with recriminations that were often severe, especially on the part of John Frederick II. There were imprisonments and removals from office. First the Philippists were chased; later, when the tables were turned, the sympathizers of Flacius were dismissed and forced to flee. Needless to say, it was a very tragic time. Of all the controversies, the Synergistic was the most bitter and vexing.

Synergism is very similar to Semi-Pelagianism, which Luther had shown to be contrary to Scripture. Melanchthon, therefore, had revived old heretical notions by teaching that there are 3 cooperating causes in conversion: God's grace, His Word, and the assenting will of man. Human reason has always found this viewpoint appealing. It was the Formula of Concord, in its 2d article, which spoke the definitive word against this heresy, describing it fully and repudiating it unequivocally. It stated clearly:

> Holy Scriptures ascribe conversion, faith in Christ, regeneration, renewal, and all that belongs to their efficacious beginning and completion, not to the human powers of the natural free will, neither entirely, nor half, nor in any, even the least part, but *in solidum,* that is, entirely and solely, to the divine working and the Holy Spirit (FC SD, II, 25).

# III. Righteousness of Faith Before God

Historical Background:
THE OSIANDRIAN
AND STANCARIAN CONTROVERSIES

The justification of the sinner before God by faith alone without the works of the Law was the Reformation's pivotal, watershed article. This teaching is the most precious of Christianity's crown jewels. By God's grace through the imputed merits of Christ, forgiveness of sins is declared to the world, to sinners everywhere, for acceptance by faith. This is God's Gospel. By it the Christian church either stands or falls. With it, all Christian doctrine hangs together in one harmonious whole; without it, the articles of faith fall like so many dominoes. No wonder that Satan has made it the target of incessant attack from the beginning. All natural religions point man inwards, to his own attainments or supposed moral perfections, for peace with his gods; Christianity alone points him to Christ, the Lamb of God, who atoned for all sin by His perfect obedience, under the Law, fulfilling it perfectly (active obedience) and taking all guilt on Himself and suffering full punishment for all (passive obedience). He, true God and true man, the incarnate Son of God, offered Himself in our place and for our sakes that we might have peace with God (Rom. 5:1).

Knowing the tendency of human nature, Luther forecast that this article would not long remain in its simple purity and clarity. It had come to light again out of the terrible confusion of Romanist distortions which placed the emphasis on the penitential works and exercises imposed on the faithful. For these Christ's sacrifice was to supply power. Again and again, especially in his commentaries on Galatians and on Genesis, Luther warned of the impending attacks Satan would make on

Christianity's central article of God's free grace in Christ. Death had barely taken him when his predictions began to be fulfilled. Since then, generations of men have found the "blood theology" of Christ's atoning sacrifice an offensive, repugnant teaching. It is bound to be so, since man's pride and human reason oppose it. How can that be congenial which insults pride and reason? Nothing else explains the continuing affront that modern theology takes from the Gospel.

Chief perpetrator of the confusion and trouble that soon arose was Osiander. Most of his ministry, from 1522 to 1548, had been spent at Nuernberg. He was a gifted, eloquent man but also found it hard to swallow other men's triumphs or recognition. While Luther was alive this problem was small, since Osiander was overshadowed by Luther theologically and intellectually. But trouble began after the Augsburg Interim (1548). Osiander had resigned his pastorate at Nuernberg, taking refuge in Koenigsberg under the patronage of an old friend, Count Albrecht of Prussia. Almost immediately the count appointed him to the post of first professor of theology at the university, though he lacked the necessary academic qualifications. This affront to other ranking theologians, including the redoubtable Moerlin, who was pastor at Koenigsberg's cathedral church, would have been tolerable; but Osiander took it as his particular mission in life to stand on the opposite side of most issues. To do this on the Reformation's central article, however, and to declare openly his opposition to and superiority over Luther on this question, was to invite sharp rebuttal and censure.

Osiander had particularly drawn a bead on the Reformation's accent on the forensic sense of justification, the teaching that God for Christ's sake declares sinners righteous. To him justification was not an act by which God *declares* sinners righteous but an act by which God gradually *makes* a man just by dwelling in him. He argued that Christ the man was righteous because of the indwelling divine nature; therefore we are justified by faith because faith unites us with the divine nature, and God's righteousness becomes ours in this way. We are not saved, said Osiander, by what Luther called alien, foreign, or imputed righteousness, the righteousness of Christ which is *outside* of us and imputed to us by faith; we are saved by the inward righteousness, the righteousness which is worked in us, as when a medicine gradually works its healing or cleansing. Justification thus is a gradual *process,* a subjective change that goes on in us. Luther had clearly emphasized that we *must* say that we are *pronounced* righteous by grace. But Osiander said that the human nature of Christ is only a kind of link or connection through which the divine nature with its essential righteousness, wisdom, and power is channeled to the believer. His was a kind of "incarnational theology." It reasons that as Christ realized His divine potential by the union of the Son of God with the human nature, so we, too, by faith in Christ are to realize our divine potential, by God being in us and by our sharing in the divine.

Osiander's theologizing was intensely subjectivistic, mystical, metaphysical, personalistic. Though he denied that good works justified a man, he insisted that it was the indwelling, progressive righteousness, which came by faith and which became more and more perfect, that saved the sinner. Even Romanist theologians recognized the similarity between his thinking and theirs. Lutheran theologians from both sides of the aisle were quick to challenge him. Melanchthon and his followers remonstrated strongly against him; so did Moerlin, Flacius, and the strongly conservative side; the milder Brenz also felt that Osiander was wrong, though he preferred to think that it was chiefly a word-hassle and a confusion of terms. But it was more than a dispute about words. Osiander was already confusing the two natures in the person of Christ, the concurring activity of both natures in the redemption of mankind, and the doctrine of the Lord's Supper, which he held to be a means whereby *we* become body and blood with Christ and part of the divine.

Osiander died 1552 at Koenigsberg at the height of the controversy. But the dissension went on. Men like Moerlin were forced to leave. But the repudiation of the heresy was general, throughout Lutheran lands. Some of the opposition, however, was of dubious value. For example, one of Osiander's colleagues, Stancarus (an ex-priest from Mantua, Italy, whose name had been Francesco Stancaro) differed with Osiander on the question of whether it was the divine nature or the human nature of Christ that effected our redemption. He taught that it was the human nature alone. Both Osiander and Stancarus were wrong. Christ works our atonement and is our Mediator according to both natures, inseparably united since the incarnation.

Stancarus meanwhile bumped around from place to place

and country to country in Europe, never able to win any following for his controversial, often bizarre, views. Though he professed support for the Reformation, he favored Peter the Lombard over Luther. Because he spread his false views widely in his travels, the writers of the Formula of Concord found it necessary to repudiate his theological ideas along with those of Osiander in Article III.

Since at this same time confusion reigned (especially among some of the clergy in Hamburg) on whether both the active obedience of Christ (whereby He was under the Law for us and perfectly fulfilled its requirements) and the passive obedience (His suffering and death) availed for our redemption, the Formula affirmed the historic and Reformation teaching that Christ is our Righteousness according to His entire person, both divine and human natures, by which he fulfills the Law of God perfectly for us even unto death, fulfilling His heavenly Father's will in every way throughout His life, and suffering and dying in our stead, for our sin.

# IV. Of Good Works

Historical Background:
THE MAJORISTIC CONTROVERSY

While this controversy bears the name of Major, its beginnings were already present in Melanchthon. Major had been a student and devoted follower of Melanchthon. He became professor at Wittenberg, and for a time, a few years before Luther's death, he served as rector, or presiding officer, of the university.

The Majoristic controversy also impinges on the article concerning justification. At stake is the connection of good works with salvation. Some theologians were teaching that good works are necessary to salvation. Melanchthon first used that expression as early as 1535, in his emended *Loci*, or dogmatics. Ostensibly his main objective was to obviate what has often been called "cheap grace," that a regenerate man, or believer, could lead a reckless, godless life, with no concern for pleasing God with his life. Profession of faith with the mouth ought after all be matched by a Christian life.

However, as Melanchthon stated the case and persistently defended it, good works were *essential* to salvation, that is, as a contributing factor or cause; for if they were absent, he argued, then no man could be saved. What he should have said, is that good works are the necessary *fruit* of justifying faith; and where such faith is present, there good works will inevitably also blossom. So, while it was perfectly correct to say that good works were necessary, it was completely incorrect to state that they were *necessary for salvation*. Jesus many times refers to faith which saves, and to good works which are the evidence of that faith, as for example in the case of the woman who "loved much" (Luke 7:47, 50). So do His apostles. "By grace are ye saved, through faith; and that not of yourselves; it is the gift of God, not of works, lest any man should boast," the apostle Paul wrote (Eph. 2:8-9). In the very next verse the same apostle stresses that these good works, which are God's "workmanship" in us, are also the *God-expected result,* "which God hath before ordained that we should walk in them" (v. 10). So, the question could not be *whether* good works were necessary, expected, or even commanded by God. Our sanctification was the will of God (1 Thess. 4:3). The question rather was: Should they be described as *necessary to salvation,* as Melanchthon began doing from 1535 onwards?

Luther cautioned him several times against using that misleading phrase. Melanchthon agreed that it could be misunderstood and that he should therefore modify it. But he remained ambivalent, willing only to admit that the words could be misunderstood, not that they were wrong in themselves. At the time of the Augsburg and Leipzig Interims when Catholic pressure was on him, he clearly was hedging and fudging on this whole matter of the relation of good works to salvation. But thereafter he often said that the expression "good works are necessary to salvation" was open to abuse and, therefore, ought to be abandoned. Obviously he wanted to avoid at all costs the Romanist teaching that good works *merit* salvation. He could have cleared up the whole confusion, if he had admitted that, as first phrased, the expression was faulty and wrong theology; and that what he should have said is that good works are the necessary fruits that flow from faith. But he never backed down on his first version or formulation. As a result many of his followers continued to use and defend it.

Foremost among the exponents of Melanchthon's point of view was Major. He had sided with his mentor for some time; but it was chiefly from the time of the Interims that he openly espoused Melanchthon's wording that good works are necessary to salvation—not because they merit or effect forgiveness of sins, he admitted, but in order that salvation, achieved by grace, might be preserved and not lost by disobedience. So, such works were necessary, if salvation was to be retained.

His critics—and there were many, from both sides, Flacius, Amsdorf, and others from the conservative side and even Melanchthon from the mediating party!—were quick to point out that he was detracting from God's grace and Christ's meritorious sacrifice, if he maintained that either justification, or salvation, or the preservation in faith and in grace, were dependent to any degree or extent on good works. Major understood what they were saying and attempted various revisions; but he, too, like Melanchthon before him, would admit only the infelicity of the phrase, that it was open to misunderstanding, rather than that it was fundamentally wrong.

It was more than dispute over words. The central article of the Bible, and of the Reformation, concerning the sinner's justification before God, was once more at stake. Major's friends knew this; but despite their admonitions he persisted and thereby aggravated the already sharp controversy.

After an interval, during which he was superintendent in Eisleben (1552), Major again became professor at Wittenberg (1553). He retained this post until his death in 1574. During all this time Major defended his original position, though he was forced to modify his views considerably, especially in the public arena.

Others had meanwhile come to Major's side. They also failed to understand the gravity of describing good works as necessary to salvation. Notable among them was Menius, superintendent at Gotha for a time; he resigned his position 1554 as a result of pressure against him for his support of Major. Menius had also supported the Interims. By itself this action was damning as far as loyal Lutherans were concerned. But taking Major's side made matters worse. Menius, too, wanted to avoid at all costs the implication that good works merited salvation, the Romanist position. So, under pressure he modified his language, but like Major and Melanchthon he only admitted its ambiguity.

The word "necessary" was bound to draw attention. Opponents of Major and Menius pointed out that the term "necessary" was harmless, as long as good works, new obedience, or renewal of life, were understood as necessary *fruits of faith*. They were also ready to stress the divine command for such new life. Coercion and compulsion were never to be associated with what had to be done spontaneously, voluntarily, freely, and willingly. So, while the apostle Paul excludes good works as a cause of salvation or justification, he fills his epistles with exhortations to good works, to earnest striving after them, and to putting down of the old sinful flesh.

Both sides appealed to Luther's authority. Early in the Reformation Luther had emphasized good works as an inevitable fruit of faith. He wrote a special treatise, *On Good*

*Works* (1520). "Faith active in love" is a continuing theme in his writings. But he also repeatedly emphasized that good works follow *after* faith and do not bear in *any* way on justification. We must labor to be outwardly righteous also, Luther stated, but this righteousness does not commend us before God (cf. *LW,* 27, 72). Here only the merits of Christ avail. Thank God it is so! Otherwise no man would ever know when he had done enough, or when his fund of grace was sufficient. But faith has all when it lays hold on God's grace in Christ. Eloquently Luther laid this "theology of the cross" *(theologia crucis)* before his fellow Augustinian friars at the Heidelberg Disputation as early as 1518. Here, too, he had pointed out that a man's good works, however shiny they might be, become injurious to a man's salvation, *if* he *trusts* in them.

Luther's good friend Amsdorf entered the fray against Major and Menius but swung the pendulum to the other extreme, asserting that good works were injurious to salvation. He wanted to capture one of Luther's emphases but failed to state the matter clearly or correctly. He should have maintained that good works, *if trusted in,* are injurious to a man's eternal salvation. But he gave only half the story, and, as a result, was severely rebuked by men like Flacius.

When the Formula of Concord settled the issue it spoke to both extremes, as well as the Antinomian notion which challenged speaking of good works as necessary at all (see Chapter V). Theologians like Agricola—notorious because of his part in the Augsburg Interim—and pastors Poach (Erfurt) and Otto (Nordhausen) held that since good works are to be done freely and out of love they must not be described as necessary. Further, they argued, the Law no longer plays any role in the Christian's life. The regenerate man, so went the argument, does not need to have the good works named or taught, for by faith he does them spontaneously and without instruction. The Formula saw the need to defend good works as necessary in the Christian's life because God commands them; this view will be dealt with more fully under the next article.

Article IV became very useful, clearly delineating the nature of good works and their relationship to faith and salvation and precisely distinguishing between justification and sanctification and between Law and Gospel.

# v. Of the Law and the Gospel

Historical Background:
THE ANTINOMISTIC CONTROVERSY

Christianity has been plagued, without letup, by one besetting problem in particular: failure to distinguish properly between Law and Gospel. These two doctrines are the chief content of the Bible. The Law is the teaching concerning man's obligation under the holy will of God: how he is to live and conduct himself and what he is to do or not do; the Gospel is the teaching of what God has done for our sakes through Christ. The Law differs from the Gospel, says Luther, as a demand laid upon us differs from a gift given to us. Walther remarked in this connection: "For the man who does not understand this distinction the Bible is a tightly locked and sealed book; but whoever understands this distinction has the key by which the Holy Scriptures alone is unlocked" (*Der Concordienformel Kern und Stern*, p.35).

Luther's study of the epistles of Paul, especially Galatians, on which he lectured several times, was the key that helped him clarify this distinction between Law and Gospel in brilliantly clear manner. Walther, in turn, drew heavily on Luther's lectures on Galatians. It was the springboard for his famous lecture series *The Proper Distinction Between Law and Gospel*. Luther had stated that since the fall the Law, in its principal, theological, or spiritual use, has the function of revealing or pressing home man's sinful condition to him. It is the "hammer of death, the thundering of hell, and the lightning of God's wrath," by which alone the "adamant wall" or "opinion of righteousness" in man can be mollified and crushed. What it did at Mt. Sinai for the Israelites, who were all "spit and polish" with outward preparations as they waited before God, the Law continues to do till this day with the pretension of righteousness that lodges in the pith and marrow of all men by nature. It smashes it to pieces. But when it has done this, "here it hath an end, and it ought to go no further" At that point a man needs to hear the Gospel, "the preaching of the free remission of sins for Christ's sake." The Gospel is "a light which lighteneth, quickeneth, comforteth, and raiseth up fearful minds, if they believe that by His death they are delivered from the curse, that is to say, from sin and everlasting death." When this distinction between the Law and Gospel is observed, "we give to them both their own proper use and office," Luther notes (*A Commentary on St. Paul's Epistle to the Galatians* [Westwood, N. J., n. d.], pp. 299—302), and this is an office and function that continues throughout the believer's life.

The root meaning of "antinomianism" is opposition to the Law. In the theological arena this "anti-Law" stance opposes the Law of God as a continuing force in a believer's life. The theory is that, once a man is regenerate and has come to faith, he no longer has need for the Law's punishing directives. True contrition and repentance, even knowledge of sin, so goes the thinking, are worked by the Gospel only. By experiencing the kindness and mercy of God the regenerate man is caused to grieve over his sins and repents.

This was the view Agricola taught and peddled. He had become a follower of Luther in the early stages of the Reformation and was present with Luther at the famous Leipzig debate in 1519. In 1525 he became teacher and preacher in Eisleben, and his long association with this town explains one of the nicknames he bore, "Eisleben." Other nicknames were less commendatory, reflecting usually his personality quirks. As events showed, he was a jealous, vain, scheming, and insincere conniver. Because Melanchthon, rather than he, received the appointment to the new theological professorship at the University of Wittenberg in 1526, Agricola nursed a permanent grudge against his erstwhile friend, as well as against Luther, who was chiefly responsible for Melanchthon's being chosen.

The first evidence of the bad blood between Agricola and Wittenberg's two noted theologians came in his printed criticism of Melanchthon's instructions for the pastors and teachers in Saxony on the proper distinction between Law and Gospel. Agricola took an extremely antinomistic position, virtually rejecting out of hand the whole Old Testament, as well as all injunctions of the Law in the lives of the regenerate.

Luther was able to resolve this unfortunate and unpleasant situation by getting Agricola to modify his extreme statements.

But Agricola never really dropped his antinomian notions and his deep feelings of jealousy and animosity against Luther and Melanchthon. In a covert way he wrote letters and published theses that were intended to undermine Luther and his teaching. It did not help matters that Melanchthon had as early as 1527 used expressions similar to those of Agricola, even stating that the Gospel was a preaching of contrition and condemnation of sin. Apparently he had merely used the term "Gospel" in its wide sense, that is, to include the whole word of God, both Law and Gospel, a usage in tune with Scripture. Luther recognized this and at times expressed himself the same way, though the context always made it plain that he was not confusing Law and Gospel.

After Luther's death Melanchthon came under fire from men like Flacius for apparently ambiguous statements; but again he convinced his adversaries that he had used "Gospel" in its wide sense rather than the narrow, proper, more usual sense. But Melanchthon's followers did not make this distinction. They insisted that the Gospel in its narrow, proper sense worked contrition and rebuked sin. Accordingly, Flacius, Amsdorf, Wigand, and many others found occasion to object to a teaching like this, which was transforming the sweet Gospel of God's forgiveness through Christ into a thundering of the Law.

Between 1537 and 1540 Luther composed 6 sets of theses against Agricola and antinomianism. Four were delivered in public disputation. Luther's patience was indeed amazing, considering the circumstances, because Agricola inevitably returned to his old position. Painstakingly Luther showed how the law continues to work contrition and knowledge of sin, even in Christians, and he pointed out that this was a necessary function if faith was to receive forgiveness and gladly accept Christ. "For who could know," Luther asked, "what and for what purpose Christ has suffered for us, if no one were to know what sin or the Law is?" "Therefore," Luther went on, "the Law must certainly be preached if we would preach Christ." This was from Luther's public letter, 1538, in which he gave assurance of Agricola's professed change of mind on the matter. (Quoted in F. Bente's Hist. Intr., *Concordia Triglotta*, p. 167.)

The case against Agricola, however, was not settled until the Elector of Saxony brought proceedings against him for false charges and calumnies leveled against Luther. But before Agricola could be tried, he moved away to Berlin. Elector Joachim of Brandenburg now interceded for him, seeking peaceful settlement of the dispute with Luther. Agricola again agreed to modify his extreme view; but it was a tongue-in-cheek affair, no more sincere than his earlier assurances. His true self really came to the fore after Luther was dead. He gained a leading role in writing the infamous Augsburg Interim (1548). Then it became evident that his faulty theology involved more than distinction between Law and Gospel. When this distinction is lost, other articles also become involved; for example, the distinction between justification and sanctification, the nature of original sin, free will, and conversion. Agricola was not only a vain, small person but a confused theologian as well; indeed he was more an opportunist than theologian.

Article V in the Formula of Concord addresses the question of the proper distinction of Law and Gospel in accord with Scripture and the Augsburg Confession. Agricola, of course, was neither the first nor the last to confuse the distinction. By nature every man inclines to confuse Law and Gospel. There seems to be an inherent propensity on man's part to make the one into the other, or try to make the Gospel do what only the Law can do and make the Law do what only the Gospel can do. Thus in Luther's own day Ulrich Zwingli, another leading Reformation figure, had stated: "In itself the Law is nothing else than a Gospel." In our day the noted Reformed theologian Karl Barth took a similar position, just as confusing and just as wrong: "The Law is the necessary form of the Gospel whose content is grace." This is to lose sight of a most important Scriptural distinction, as Luther pointed out, namely, that it is the function of the Law to kill, smash, destroy, and the function of the Gospel to lift up, quicken, give life. (2 Cor. 3:6) Never do the twain meet. Never do their functions fuse. Law and Gospel continue through life to have their distinctive and necessary functions also for the regenerate man. The Gospel can only be preached effectively in the context of the Law, that is, where the Law has smashed self-righteous pretension. Conversely, only where faith reigns through the Gospel is the power for love of God and and one's fellowman in accord with God's holy will, the Law.

# VI. Of the Third Use of the Law

Historical Background:
THE ANTINOMISTIC CONTROVERSY

There was another side to the antinomistic controversy. Agricola found, at least temporarily, new prestige and power through his collaboration with the Interimists, the party that was ready to compromise doctrine for the sake of peace with the emperor and the Romanists. With new brazenness he peddled his views far and wide, spouting of how the Law belongs in the state house or the judge's chambers, while the Christian believer should pay attention to the Gospel only. With a cheery sort of confidence Agricola quoted Luther as saying: "The greatest knowledge in the world for a believer is not to know the Law." Luther indeed had said as much and did mean it very sincerely; for in the matter of justification it was most important that a sinner look only to the cross, to Christ, to God's forgiveness, to His promise of grace. But Luther just as clearly supported the continued use and principal function of the Law to work the knowledge of sin and contrition, so that the Gospel can find entrance in the convicted sinner's heart. And he never denied the continuing significance of the Law in the sinner's life as a guide to godly living and behavior.

It was on this latter point that some of Agricola's sympathizers, especially the Philippists, put special emphasis. The main issue now was not whether the Law was necessary to work contrition and prepare the soil in men's hearts and lives for the advent of the Gospel, but whether the Law was necessary as a guide or rule in the lives of believers. In other words, besides the political use (curb) and the primary theological use (mirror or hammer), was there also a 3d use of the Law as pattern or guide? In the new obedience, or renewal of life, which results from faith in the justified man, is the Law really still necessary or at all applicable?

This was the question, and around it another controversy swirled for a time.

Leaders in this dissension were Poach, pastor in Erfurt; Otto, pastor in Nordhausen; Musculus, professor and pastor, later also superintendent, at Frankfurt an der Oder; and Michael Neander, friend of Otto and pastor at Ilfeld. It was first of all Poach's rejoinder (1556) against the extreme views of Major (who stipulated that good works are necessary to salvation) which led to the beginning of what is known as the 2d antinomistic controversy. Poach held that the Law had no place at all in the church, at least among regenerate believers; even if a man were to keep the Law perfectly and completely he could not be justified by this. Otto, on the other hand, stressed merely the Law's discontinuance for the Christian as a teaching norm, holding that the believer by faith spontaneously knows and does what is God-pleasing. Musculus had similar views.

Poach later changed his position and signed the Formula of Concord, thereby recognizing the error of his position as spelled out in the 5th and 6th articles. Musculus, too, was involved more with an error of the mind than of the heart. Not too many years later he was one of the theologians who helped to put the "Bergic Book," the Solid, or Thorough, Declaration of the Formula, into final shape. Otto likewise came to see that he was less than discreet in his wording, for he recognized that, when Luther spoke of "not knowing the Law" as the "greatest knowledge" for a Christian, the Reformer was referring to justification, not sanctification. So, the excesses to which these men came in some of their statements can in large measure be explained as overreaction to the error of Major and others who insisted on good works as necessary to salvation. Their reflex action was to deemphasize the Law to the point of denying its continuing significance or relevance in the life of a believing sinner altogether.

Such disparagement of the Law was out of character with Scripture and the Augsburg Confession. The writers of the Formula of Concord wanted to nail this down very tight. There was good reason for such concern. Whenever the Law or the Gospel or both in their respective spheres have been attacked and threatened, it has worked to the eventual detriment of both. When in the name of the Gospel, or the freedom of the Gospel, or the love of Christ an attack is leveled against the pertinence of the Law, both in its accusatory function and/or its informatory function as a teaching norm, it is inevitable that the Gospel itself ends up being twisted and distorted as well. In fact, the great tragedy is that the Gospel is then lost! F. Bente has observed with keen discernment that "the cocoon of antinomianism always bursts into antigospelism" (*Concordia Triglotta,* Hist. Intr., p. 161).

It is ironic—and yet not strange when one remembers how cleverly Satan works to subvert the Gospel in every century—that Lutherans should be haggling over the question of whether or not Luther ever really taught the 3d use of the Law. In raising the question and doubt in people's minds, the hope apparently is to throw a new, more Gospel-oriented hue over the 6th article of the Formula of Concord. This is more than a dangerous word game. The Gospel itself will be turned into a new "law."

The Formula of Concord lays out the uses of the Law in a threefold way, so that there will be no misunderstanding. The Christian, because of the old sinful nature inherent in him till he dies, has need for the curbing function of the Law, the mirroring (or hammering) function above all, and also the teaching or guiding function (lest he adopt a self-conceived program of so-called holiness).

Throughout his life, throughout his writings, Luther underscores each of these functions. Whether he uses the *term* "third use of the Law" cannot be the issue. As he so often said when embroiled in controversy, importance attaches to the *thing* termed, not the term. There are dozens of places in his lectures on Galatians where Luther carefully shows the connection between justification and sanctification, and demonstrates how faith inevitably bears fruit in good works and thus is never alone. In connection with this he indicates how the Law functions as the guide for Christian living in the believer's life. So, it is the mark of a "saint," or believer, that he not only believe in and have Christ as his righteousness—by which he alone is saved—but that he also "do his duty in his vocation," says Luther, "according to the rule of God's Word *(ex praescripto Verbi),*" that is, according to the prescription of the Word.

Those who deny that Luther, or the Lutheran Confessions, taught the Third Use of the Law have no leg to stand on. It is important for Christians to recognize the value of the Law in their lives as God's teaching instrument, understanding always that neither motivation nor power to keep the commandments lie in or with the Law but in God's precious Gospel and faith.

# VII. Of the Lord's Supper and
# VIII. Of the Person of Christ

## Historical Background:
## CRYPTO-CALVINISTIC CONTROVERSY

Misrepresentation, speaking with forked tongue, was the name of the game in the Crypto-Calvinistic Controversy. The term itself indicates that "hidden Calvinism" was insinuating itself into the Lutheran church and Lutheran theology. It was never a concern of the Lutheran churches to remain Lutheran for Lutheranism's sake alone, but for the sake of Christianity, for the sake of basic Scriptural truths. When Luther said of Zwingli and Bucer that they had a different spirit, he pinpointed a tendency towards rationalism which regrettably has characterized much theologizing in the church, especially Reformed theology. Eventually crucial articles like the Lord's Supper and the doctrine of the person of Christ came to be affected by rationalism's judgments.

On basis of Scripture Luther had contended over against the Sacramentarians that Christ's true body and blood were the real, substantial gift which God bestows upon the communicants—worthy or unworthy—in the Lord's Supper. The words of Christ, "Take eat, this is My body *which is given for you*," confirm this. In, with, and under bread and wine in the Sacrament the communicant receives Christ's true body and blood. This sacramental presence was not to be understood merely as spiritual, but truly real, though supernatural, effected by the mighty power of God through His Word. Luther made no attempt to explain *how* God could accomplish what He promised; but he resisted every attempt to reduce what Christ so plainly bestowed as the seal of the forgiveness of sins in the Sacrament, namely, His body and blood. The apostle Paul likewise taught the Real Presence in clear, unambiguous terms (1 Cor. 10:16; 11:23-29).

It was not only the Sacrament that came under fire. The person of Christ also became a target for rationalistic reductionism by Zwingli and Calvin and their followers. The problem, or question, was: How could the infinite majesty of God, with all the divine attributes reside within the man Jesus Christ? Calvin consistently upheld the God-man status of Jesus Christ. But, on basis of the principle that the finite is not capable of the infinite, Calvinism had also just as consistently denied the full communication of divine attributes to Christ according to His human nature. Thus, although Scripture attests that *all* power, wisdom, and omnipresence were given, communicated, or bestowed upon Him, Reformed theologians have regularly considered such bestowal to be of limited scope, that is, that Christ possesses the divine prerogatives only according to His divine nature. Now, it is true that during the time of His earthly sojourn Christ for the most part limited the full *use* of these divine excellencies, according to His human nature, in order that He might accomplish His saving mission. But as to *possession* of the fulness of the divine majesty and Godhead, also according to his human nature, Scripture leaves no doubt. Paul states in a summary, propositional way: "In Him dwelleth all the fulness of the Godhead bodily" (Col. 2:9). Accordingly, Lutheran theology repudiates as false and unscriptural the Calvinistic teaching that the ascended Christ is to be limited according to His human nature to a localized inclusion or seclusion at the right hand of God.

Luther remonstrated against such delimiting of Christ's power, stating that the right hand of God is everywhere; it is the right hand of power, and Scriptures surely teach that Christ, the undivided God-man fulfills His promise to be everywhere literally. Dimensions of space, time, and motion, are not impediments—not even as regards His human nature—for Him who is the almighty God. Therefore, in the Sacrament there is no insuperable hurdle which Christ must overcome to give us His true body and blood in His own supernatural, almighty way.

It goes without saying that the doctrine of the person of Christ impinged closely on the Lord's Supper, and vice versa. Lutherans who upheld the full bestowal of divine attributes to Christ according to His human nature, from the time of His wonderful incarnation, found perfect agreement in this with His promise of His true body and blood in the Lord's Supper. Calvinists, on the other hand, denying that the divine attributes could be held or contained within the human nature, have denied also that Christ's body and blood are actually present and given in the Lord's Supper.

Compromise statements, which used the familiar words but shielded beneath them the meaning of the Calvinist position, had appeared even before Luther's death. These were without success in bringing the two factions of Protestantism together. In fact, Luther had expressed concern, shortly before departure on the last trip of his life to Eisleben, that members of the Wittenberg faculty had been infected with Calvinist leaven on the Lord's Supper. So he announced that there would be an across-the-board examination of the staff upon his return. As God willed, he died suddenly at Eisleben. In any case it is clear that he surmised that the seeds of a "spiritualized" or "symbolical" mode of Christ's presence in the Sacrament had infiltrated the Wittenberg faculty. As time showed, he was not wrong. In due course the Philippists began to show how "soft" they were on this question and how ready to compromise with the Calvinists.

Calvin had revealed in his acceptance of the *Consensus of Zurich,* also called the *Consensus Tigurinus* (1549), that his position and that of Zwingli on the Lord's Supper were compatible. For most Lutherans this reinforced what they had always understood, namely, that Reformed theologians, no matter how they worded it, accepted only a spiritual presence of Christ in the Sacrament. The fact that there were some on the Wittenberg faculty who were willing to accede to this document showed that Luther's fears were not unfounded. Towards the end of Luther's life Melanchthon had expressed increasing regard and sympathy for Calvin's view on some points of the doctrinal cleavage. Yet on the Lord's Supper he had usually been consistent in defending the Lutheran position, at least in public conclaves, e.g., at Wittenberg in 1536, at Smalcald in 1537, and in his public statements after the death of Luther.

But Melanchthon was different from Luther when it came to outspoken, frank avowal of inward thoughts. Luther always wore his heart on his sleeve. Never did he leave any man in doubt as to where he stood. His word was as true as gold. Melanchthon, however, was the vacillator, the oscillator, on the fence; his cogitations, sometimes worries, augured more than a storm in a tea cup. Thus even his silence, while the Philippists were stirring the Calvinistic brew under his nose at Wittenberg, was really unforgivable. Had Luther been alive, short shrift would have been made of the troublemakers. But Melanchthon dillydallied. He was no longer convinced of the literal sense and interpretation of the words of institution of the Lord's Supper, and he likewise was not sure about the Lutheran position on Christ's omnipresence according to His human nature. His part in the Interims underscored the fact that his old humanistic rationalism was still alive and a menace to the Lutheran cause. The fact that he also vehemently opposed champions of Lutheran orthodoxy and sympathized with the parties that stood for compromise, whether Romanist or Reformed, reinforced the judgment of his critics against him. Thus his rapport was probably better with Calvin and with a compromiser like Martin Bucer than with men loyal to Luther's position.

One of the earliest orthodox Lutheran pastors to speak out against the encroaching pro-Calvinistic interpretation of the Lord's Supper was Westphal of Hamburg. As early as 1552 he noted how deep was the inroad into Lutheran churches and theology. Others, like Chemnitz and Moerlin, took a stand against Hardenberg, pastor in Bremen, for his Crypto-Calvinism.

But in Wittenberg the tide flowed towards compromise. Melanchthon was either too tired, too unconcerned, or too unsure to do anything about the pro-Calvinist tendencies. The theologians on the staff were almost all of the same compromising tendencies; and the two ringleaders, Melanchthon's son-in-law, Kaspar Peucer, professor of medicine, and personal physician for Prince August, and Georg Cracow, professor of jurisprudence and personal counselor to the Elector, were able to gain the ear of their patron and sympathy for the "new theology" in Wittenberg.

The Philippists convinced their prince that "Melanchthonian Lutheranism" was the real and genuine article, particularly on the Lord's Supper and the person of Christ, and that the rival party members were what they called "Ubiquitists," who taught that Christ's body was somehow locally extended through the universe; that the latter were the real troublemakers, obstructionists, legalists, Biblicists, literalists, out of touch with reality, etc. Under aegis of the elector they published their *Corpus Doctrinae,* which included the altered Augsburg Confession and altered Apology, a preface by Melanchthon, as well as the latest emended edition of Melanchthon's *Loci,* among its "confessions." Above all they were able to convince the prince that Luther's theology and writings, especially his position on the Lord's Supper and the person of Christ, were to be understood according to Melanchthon's interpretation. Melanchthon knew the real Luther and mind of Luther, they argued. This new statement was also known as the *Corpus Philippicum,* and it became the official teaching or confessional base for all Saxony.

Opposition to it was immediate and intense. Even some of the students at Wittenberg became involved, and two of them, Conrad Schluesselburg and Albert Schirmer, were expelled for leveling charges of false doctrine against members of the faculty. But whole faculties throughout Lutheran lands, including those in Saxony, like Jena and Weimar, also stood opposed. Elector August sought for peace and amity through mutual discussion and convocations, but to no avail. His "trusted" faculty at Wittenberg persuaded him to go on thinking that they were indeed the guarantors of orthodox Lutheran teaching, loving, and Gospel-oriented, and that the others were reactionaries.

What transpired in Wittenberg was duplicated in other Lutheran territories, some of which were eventually and entirely lost to the Lutheran cause, as in the Palatinate (Heidelberg). But elsewhere there was stiff, knowledgeable resistance. Moerlin and Chemnitz, among others, were successful in withstanding the influx of the Calvinistic view on the Sacrament in northern Germany, particularly against a confirmed pro-Calvinist like Pastor Hardenberg of Bremen. Yet the sympathies in this famous free city of the old Hanseatic League still were for the most part against the strict Lutheran position. In Wuerttemberg it was Brenz who became the stalwart defender of the Real Presence of Christ's true body and blood in the Sacrament. There were many others, for example, Chytraeus in Rostock and Andreae at the University of Tuebingen, in Swabia. It was Moerlin who gave the lie to the "Heidelberg Fable" *(Heidelberg Landluege)* which portrayed Luther as having confessed to Melanchthon late in his life that he probably had been too severe in his castigation of the Sacramentarians and the Calvinistic position on the Lord's Supper.

The Altenburg Colloquy between the dissenting parties, which Elector August had called, lasted from Oct. 1568 to March 1569, and ended in a triumph for the Crypto-Calvinists. The elector viewed them as the loyal, loving, evangelical party, and the others as the irascible troublemakers. Step for step the efforts now became more bold. In 1570 the Wittenberg Philippists published *Propositions Concerning the Chief Controversies of This Time,* a blatant denial of the strictly Lutheran teaching on the Lord's Supper and the full majesty of Christ's person according to His human nature. They followed this in 1571 with a catechism that fostered the same view. In Wittenberg they even published a piece written by a Jesuit which was critical of Andreae, one of Lutheran theology's most loyal sons.

To show that they were completely "ecumenical," the Philippists showed favor to the arch-Calvinist and successor to Calvin, Theodore Beza, by reprinting one of his books in Wittenberg; and he, in turn, very tactfully, with a stroke of diplomatic genius, dedicated it to Elector August. Meanwhile, their intrigue to take over the Saxon territories entirely was given great stimulus by the death of John William, ruler of ducal Saxony and a staunch Lutheran; Elector August, of electoral Saxony, became the guardian for his two young sons. The Wittenberg Crypto-Calvinistic Philippists moved swiftly. They persuaded the elector to rid both Saxon territories of all the Ubiquitists or Flacianists, all who refused to subscribe the *Corpus Philippicum* of 1560. More than a hundred Lutheran theologians, pastors, and teachers were affected and forced to leave their positions, homes, and land.

The Calvinistic take-over was all but complete. But the plotters, led by Peucer, wanted to make things double sure. In 1574 they published, anonymously and without indication of place or date of publication, a document entitled *Exegesis perspicua,* or "Clear Explanation," which clearly supported the Calvinist position, denigrated some of Luther's statements and writings, and urged fellowship and union of Lutheran and Reformed churches. The latter was not inconceivable, since the distinctive Lutheran positions had been surrendered. With opposition within his territories now practically silenced, the elector received urgent criticisms from churchmen, princes, and others throughout the Lutheran world. But by and large he turned a deaf ear to these warnings, trusting his Wittenberg faculty and advisers.

But then the roof fell in on the schemers who swore allegiance to the Lutheran Confessions on the one hand and on the other worked for their undoing. A letter of Peucer miscarried or was misdirected. He had written to the "wife of the court preacher," intending it for the wife of the Crypto-Calvinist pastor, Christian Schuetze. In it he had urged her to give the enclosed Calvinistic prayerbook to Anna, the wife of Elector August; and he added slyly: "If first we have Mother Anna on our side, there will be no difficulty in winning His Lordship (August) too." But the letter got into the hands of the wife of another preacher at the prince's court, Lysthenius. It was in Latin. She handed it over to her husband for translation. When he saw what was involved, he immediately delivered it to the elector, whose eyes were finally opened. He understood in a flash the massive intrigue, doublespeak, dishonesty, and cunning dissembling that had been going on under his nose and in his realm for the last dozen years or more. The conspirators were unmasked. Piece by piece the rest of their sordid trail of betrayal of the elector's trust was laid bare. Had they admitted to their pro-Calvinist leanings and intentions, they would simply have been dismissed from their positions and let go. But persisting in their loyalty to the Lutheran Confessions they came under the elector's severest judgment and punishment.

In short order there was a thorough theological housecleaning throughout electoral and ducal Saxony. Professors and pastors who had been deposed were reinstated, and the land rejoiced over the reintroduction of Luther's writings and Lutheran theology. From this point on it was men like Andreae, Chemnitz, and Selnecker who became the trusted advisers of the elector in matters theological. And it was he, with other sympathetic laymen, princes of Lutheran territories, who expedited with favor and with funds the effort that was to lead to the "Bergic Book." Two notable articles in the latter would be those addressing the Crypto-Calvinistic threat on the Lord's Supper and the person of Christ, Articles VII and VIII. These still remain the minimal base on which every consultation or effort toward fellowship between Lutheran and Reformed bodies must proceed, if such discussions or dialogues are to be frank and forthright and hopefully lead to genuine peace and unity of faith.

# IX. Of the Descent of Christ to Hell

## Historical Background:
## CONTROVERSY ON CHRIST'S DESCENT INTO HELL

"He descended into hell." This truth is expressed in the Apostles' Creed and in the Athanasian Creed. In both, the descent into hell is placed after Christ's death and burial, and before His triumphant resurrection from the grave. The Lutheran Confessions echo and affirm the same fact in the Augsburg Confession, Art. III, "Of the Son of God"; in the Smalcald Articles, Part I; and in the Small and Large Catechisms. Scriptural authority for this event in Christ's life is 1 Pet. 3:18-20 and Col. 2:15. In an oft-quoted sermon at Torgau, 1533, Luther also noted Ps. 16 and Acts 2:24, 27.

In that sermon Luther stressed the fact that it was the person of Christ, undivided, who went to hell; that, in other words, it was not merely His soul which was involved, or His divine nature, but the whole Christ. Secondly, he underscored the fact that there was now no more suffering or humiliation; but that it was the triumphant Christ who declared His victory over Satan and hell. At the same time Luther cautioned that we ought not try to pry deeper into the mystery of this occurrence than we can on basis of Scripture. We know nothing beyond that; and what we know is limited primarily to the fact that it occurred, that it was triumphal, and that it was, therefore, not to be associated either with further suffering, with satisfaction of God's wrath and judgment, or with humiliation. Luther advised not to probe further into the way this event occurred and what was involved in it for the Savior.

The controversy which occurred in the Lutheran church was rather limited, gravitating around Aepinus of Hamburg. Moreover, it was practically limited to that city and its environs. It did not revive the faulty teaching of the

Scholastics, some of whom had taught that Christ's descent to hell was according to His soul only; nor the notion of Calvin and the Reformed theologians, who taught that the whole matter ought to be viewed as a figurative or symbolical expression designating Christ's intense sufferings. Aepinus, who is generally remembered for his otherwise conservative and loyal Lutheranism, was of the opinion that the descent into hell ought to be considered as the final stage in Christ's humiliation. He did not doubt that it was the whole Christ who was involved, nor did he doubt that it was a very real occurrence; but he felt that it must be considered as part of the Savior's Passion, indeed the last and climactic part.

Aepinus' colleagues and fellow clergymen in Hamburg were quick to respond. They pointed out that Christ's words from the cross "It is finished" marked the end of His vicarious suffering. The city council of Hamburg solicited a *Gutachten* from Melanchthon in 1550. He responded, referring primarily to Luther's sermon; but he failed to stress what Luther had made plain, namely, that Christ's descent as described in Holy Scripture is marked by triumph, not with further suffering, and that it thus belongs properly with His exaltation and not as the final step of His humiliation.

Melanchthon's indecisive answer caused the controversy to spread somewhat and to involve others besides the Hamburg clergy. Aepinus died in 1553, and by that time the issue was closed as far as Hamburg was concerned, since the council had forbidden further controversy on the question for the people's sake. But theologians in other Lutheran lands kept the controversy going for some time. The issue was always the same: whether Christ's descent should be viewed as involving further and final suffering, thus as part of the humiliation, or whether it belonged to His exaltation. In a few instances the controversy became intense and some proponents of views like those of Aepinus were harshly punished. To forestall further confusion, therefore, the framers of the Formula of Concord considered it wise to include a short article on the subject and therefore wrote Article IX. They were satisfied with Luther's clear statements in the Torgau sermon, among which were these salient thoughts:

> We simply believe that the entire person, God and man, after the burial, descended into hell, conquered the devil, destroyed the power of hell, and took from the

devil all his might.... But how this occurred we should not curiously investigate, but reserve until the other world, where not only this point, but also still others will be revealed, which we here simply believe, and cannot comprehend with our blind reason. (Quoted in *Concordia Triglotta,* Hist. Intr., p. 195.)

# x. Of Church Rites

Which Are Commonly Called Adiaphora or Matters of Indifference

Historical Background:
THE ADIAPHORISTIC CONTROVERSY

Second guessing the sequence of historical events is at best a hazardous pursuit, and at worst a gross distortion. What would America have been like had Abraham Lincoln been able to survive and face the difficulties in the reconstruction period himself, instead of Andrew Johnson? It is quite possible that the difficulties would have been as great, and equally possible that his great reputation as the emancipator would have been somewhat sullied. On the other hand, he might have proved equal to the task. What would things have been like in the difficult days after the Smalcald War of 1547, had Luther still been on the scene instead of Melanchthon as the leader of the Lutheran party? How would Luther have handled the Augsburg Interim, which was pressed on the defeated Lutheran forces by Emperor Charles V and composed in part by Luther's own erstwhile friend Agricola? The champion of Worms would rather have died than to have acceded to its demands, which included recognition of papal authority. And he would not have put even the dot over an "i" in a document like the Leipzig Interim, which the tremulous Melanchthon forged under heat and pressure from two political moguls, the emperor on the one side and Duke Moritz, traitor to the Lutheran cause, on the other.

Little is gained in trying to rehabilitate Melanchthon's reputation or to sully it further. He simply was not big enough for the task, and it was a horrendous one. There was nothing he could have wished for more than that Luther would have been at his side. As early as 1530 at the Diet of Augsburg, if Luther had not been prodding him constantly, buoying up his spirits, spelling out what he was to do and say, Melanchthon would have caved in. Luther, it must be remembered, had unwillingly stayed back at Castle Coburg, on the Saxon side of the border, because his prince, Elector John Frederick, fearing for his life, would not permit him to be present. After all, Luther was under the imperial edict as well as the papal ban.

True, Melanchthon had shown considerable mettle when the provisions of the Augsburg Interim first became known. He knew that compromise of the Lutheran position would involve further deterioration in doctrinal stance, eventually penetrating to the central article of the Reformation itself. But brave though his remonstrances were at first, he yielded to pressure, especially from Duke Moritz (who was now Elector, for John Frederick had been captured by the emperor and stripped of his title and lands), and drew up what he hoped would be an adequate substitute document, acceptable to both Romanists and Lutherans. After all, had not Luther also taught a certain amount of tolerance and patience on doctrinal matters at the time when the people were first making the transition from Catholicism to evangelical faith? Were there not adiaphora, that is, indifferent matters, open questions, where Christian freedom obtained and where it made no difference whether one way or one custom was preferred over another?

Melanchthon thought he could walk this thin line now, holding on to the articles of faith themselves and yielding on things like papal authority and Romish rites. But he also watered down clear-cut evangelical, Lutheran teaching on key articles in order not to offend the adversaries. When he felt threatened, Melanchthon resorted to compromise, typically a humanist and moralist rather than an erudite theologian. Not even the authority of Scripture and Luther's memory could hold back the riptide of fear that gripped him—fear for his life and for that of the churches. Nor did he have the theological backbone of Luther to remain consistent and true to Scripture under all circumstances.

The spirit of indifference and religious fellowship without doctrinal agreement (the latter sometimes called unionism) had their beginnings with Melanchthon, as far as the Lutheran church is concerned. That spirit never dies out completely, as our day has shown. Melanchthon even stooped to obsequious servility at the period of most intense pressure, stating in a pettifogging sort of letter to Elector Moritz' counselor how he had endured "a most shameful servitude" under Luther. Little could he foresee how his miserable failure at this crucial hour in Lutheran history would not only bring dishonor to the cause of the Reformation but also be the chief instrument for throwing his own church into confusion. Melanchthon became the catalyst, willing or unwilling, conscious or unwitting, for the controversies that were to vex the Lutheran church for the next 30 years.

The ultimate goal of the Augsburg Interim, a temporary measure, was to bring the Lutheran "faction" back under the papal power and control. Even though Charles V had soundly defeated the poorly prepared Lutheran forces in the Smalcald War, he knew better than to try to force too much too soon on the people of the Lutheran territories. He would have had a major uprising on his hands. So he worked on basis of a compromise, one that seemed to leave the chief Reformation articles intact while demanding compliance on papal and episcopal recognition of the bishops and hierarchy, as well as the Romish rites and sacraments. Lutherans were to be permitted some privileges, such as receiving "both kinds," bread and wine, in the Sacrament and maintaining the right of marriage for their clergy. But opposition to the Interim was intense and immediate from every quarter in Lutheran territories. Reprisals by the emperor were correspondingly severe.

In southern Germany and in the Rhine lands more than 400 clergy and their families were forced to flee. Some were imprisoned, a few were killed. The emperor used every severity to try to bend the resistance of Duke John Frederick, the deposed ruler of electoral Saxony who was his captive; but the duke did not flinch. Confessing loyalty to Scripture, he stood by the Lutheran position as expressed in the Augsburg Confession. Duke Philip of Hesse, likewise captured in the short-lived war, was not as steadfast; in exchange for freedom he agreed to comply with the Interim's demands. But his sons and the people of his territory refused to go along. North Germany likewise remained loyal, and Magdeburg for a time became the center of the resistance, as countless Lutheran leaders, among them Flacius, Gallus, and Wigand, fled there for haven. Eventually Duke Moritz, the new elector of Saxony, brought that city to its knees by a 13-month siege. Melanchthon, too, caved in, along with the Wittenberg faculty, and together they issued the still more infamous Leipzig Interim, so named from the meeting place of the next Diet later that same year (1548).

The stipulations of the Leipzig Interim were not drastically different from the Augsburg Interim. It included recognition of papal authority and Romish ceremonies, for example, in connection with Baptism (sprinkling with salt and exorcism), confirmation by bishops, extreme unction, Corpus Christi processions, and fasting rules. But worst of all was the ambivalent language on central articles like justification by faith alone, shrouding this vital Reformation article in terms acceptable to the Romanists. Melanchthon had succeeded in appeasing the enemies, but he had made many new ones among his Lutheran associates. The situation became so bad that in many locales where the faithful Lutheran pastor had been replaced by a "collaborator," the people simply refused the "intruder's" ministrations. Worst of all, the theologians, once loyal to the Reformation cause, were now split into opposing parties. On the one side were men like Melanchthon, Bugenhagen, Major, and Pfeffinger; on the other side the redoubtable Flacius, Amsdorf, Wigand, Gallus, Westphal, Aquila; and each side had their sympathizers. Lutheranism was sorely split.

The issue centered on the question of adiaphora. Under ordinary circumstances all Lutherans would have agreed that there is freedom in matters neither commanded nor forbidden by Scripture. Religious rites and customs, even the form of church government, are indifferent matters; they may be one way or another. This was the position which Melanchthon and his cohorts opted for. But Flacius quickly pointed out that in time of confession, *in casu confessionis,* when the faith itself is at stake, when persecution and threat force compliance to an authority that has shown itself to be ungodly and anti-Scriptural, then there can be no compromise. Matters like ceremonies and customs were no longer just that; they had become matters of principle and conscience, offenses to evangelical faith. When they were exacted under coercion, they were no longer free matters. Under such circumstances the central article of justification by faith alone was the prime target. The small door which was being opened was the gateway to denial of Christianity's central truth.

To appeal to Luther under such circumstances, and to urge compromise and compliance for the sake of peace, was to misread him completely. Adiaphora and indifferent matters are always subject to judgments of time and conditions. Now was a time for confession, not compromise. These were no longer indifferent matters; they were no longer "free"; nor would they effect any genuine, evangelical oneness with the opponents, but would result in a surrender of the Gospel. It was the Gospel which now was threatened, not the adiaphora, or certain customs or rites. To yield now, even though under other circumstances they might be considered indifferent matters, was really idolatrous.

To elevate external union when Christian unity of doctrine had not been attained would be grossly deceptive and untrue to God's will. It would confuse the faithful; it would destroy their faith. Luther, under such circumstances, would have advocated only one course: resistance, even if it meant loss of property and life itself. Accordingly, when it came to writing the Formula of Concord, which finally brought an end to this troublesome question, the writers quoted at length from Luther, especially from his Smalcald Articles of 1537.

The champion of the Lutheran cause at this stage was Flacius. His fearless stand and facile pen rallied the broken forces of the Lutheran cities and lands. It was a serious blow to the Lutheran cause to have Melanchthon lead the opposition, the compromise faction. His influence was still considerable. Later his reputation went into eclipse. To his credit it must be said that he admitted 1556 by letter to Flacius: "I have sinned in this matter and ask forgiveness of God." By then the Peace of Augsburg (1555) had been signed, granting Lutherans their free status before the law. But the damage had been done. Melanchthon's spirit of compromise, which had split the Lutherans widely, ran amuck in the theological strife that for years tore at the innards of the Lutheran church. It did not end until Elector August and his faithful theologians were able to present the church with a genuine platform for peace, the Formula of Concord, in 1577. Here there was no compromise, no faithless surrender of the faith, only clear attestation of the faith as it had once been confessed by their fathers at Augsburg in 1530.

The 1970s are a different day. The field is strewn with the relics and casualties of continuing religious strife and dissension among Christian bodies. The mood of our day again is for compromise and fellowship at any cost. Since Vatican II Rome has been among the leading forces for union. Protestantism is a confused medley of diluted and syncretistic strands, an amorphous ecclesiastical zoo. Under such conditions the question arises: what difference does it make that we differ in so-called nonessentials, so long as we all recognize the Lordship of Christ? Should not that be enough? When such a mood prevails it is difficult to refrain from confusing Christianity's distinctive content and message, and, above all, from losing the very heart of the evangelical truth of God's Gospel. The Formula of Concord is still an instrument which can serve as Protestantism's conscience in achieving a God-pleasing basis for fellowship and genuine unity. Walther stated it well 100 years ago:

> In view of the fact that ours is a day when religious unionism and syncretism are rife in the churches, it is this 10th article of the *Formula of Concord* which has become the veritable citadel for our time, for which we, often despised and slandered for our unswerving loyalty to the unaltered Augsburg Confession, cannot thank, praise, and exalt God enough (*Der Concordienformel Kern und Stern,* p. 25).

# XI. Of God's Eternal Foreknowledge and Election

Historical Background:
A DISPUTED SUBJECT IN CHRISTENDOM:
DIVINE ELECTION

As of 1577 dissension had not occurred on this subject. The Lutheran church after the days of Luther had been spared what could have been a very grievous situation, had dispute risen on the nature of God's election and predestination. Since Calvinism had made inroads on other articles, notably the Lord's Supper and the person of Christ, it is conceivable that Lutheran theology might also have been split into two camps on the question of man's election unto salvation. The writers of the Formula of Concord were aware of the potential threat, however, noting that while "no public dissension has occurred among the theologians of the Augsburg Confession," it was undoubtedly wise to set forth their position clearly, "lest offensive disputations concerning the same be instituted in the future" (FC, Epitome, XI, 1).

That threat was always a very real one, because of the nature of this wonderful teaching and because of the natural tendency of human reason to distort it. C. F. W. Walther, in 1877, also observed that the Lutheran camp had no division at the time (1577) when this article was incorporated into the Formula. But Walther was well aware of the threat that dispute on this article posed for the Lutheran churches in America of his day. There was considerable divergence on the question of the human will's part in conversion, and on the troublesome question of why some, to whom God's grace comes, respond in faith, while others reject it in unbelief.

Missouri and the other members of the Synodical Conference stood behind the 11th article of the Formula. In 1881

Walther published "Thirteen Theses," which epitomized that stand, and these served to heal the threatening breach among members of his synod. But the Norwegian Synod, led largely by Prof. F. A. Schmidt, who had been a member of Walther's faculty in St. Louis, broke with the Synodical Conference. Leading theologians of the Iowa Synod and the Ohio Synod also sided with the larger faction of the Norwegian Synod. Walther's opponents argued, somewhat in the tradition of Melanchthon, that there must be, at least in a small way, a contributing or assenting will on the part of man to account for the reason why some are saved and others lost. It was the synergistic answer. Walther and his followers detected this. The 11th article of the Formula was their defense. In turn, they were charged with "Crypto-Calvinism" by their opponents, a claim entirely unsupported and unsupportable, as a comparison with the Formula's article showed. The sacred purposes and acts of God have always been the target of man's remonstrances and rationalizing spirit, gracious though God is and continues to be.

As far as the Lutheran church was concerned, Luther had settled matters on this subject with his amazing rebuttal of Erasmus in the *Bondage of the Will* (1525). Man by nature is so totally corrupt that he is unable, even in the slightest, to begin or sustain any spiritual motions to improve his relationship with God. Thus his salvation is entirely dependent on and wrought by the grace of God *(sola gratia)*. Moreover, what God thus accomplishes in time, in man's lifetime, leading him to faith and salvation, is a divine purpose that is laid already in eternity. For God is sovereign in every way. There are no surprises for God in history and its events. God's will and purpose runs through all, also in man's conversion and election unto salvation. That he becomes a believing child of God is something that lies within the eternal and gracious purpose of God. No other truth in Scripture spells out more plainly the lie of synergism, the notion that man's cooperating nonresisting will is somehow a factor in his conversion.

On the other hand, Luther always followed Scripture in laying at man's door alone the sin of man's unbelief and resistance against God's grace. If a man is lost, he has only himself to blame. God's judgment falls on him in just recompense for unbelief. Luther realized fully the difficulties that the human mind has with the question why some believe and others do not believe. If God's grace is universal and He earnestly desires to save all, and if it is alone by God's grace that a man is saved, why then are not all saved? This is to try to pry into God's secret counsels, Luther cautioned. Here one must put his finger on his lips and maintain silence; for we do not know. But what we do not know now, Luther felt, we would know hereafter in glory. Meanwhile, rather than criticize God in any way for the way His divine purposes work and are seen, we should only praise Him for His unspeakable mercy and goodness, which we see and have in Christ, our Savior. Dare we speak critically of God in His gracious purpose when we don't even deserve any of it, Luther asked?

So Luther rejected on the one hand the synergistic tendencies, which traced the reason for man's salvation to something in man's own volitional capacity and, on the other hand, the answer of Calvin which solved the dilemma by positing two sovereign wills in God, one to the election of some by sovereign decree, and the other to the reprobation, or damnation, of the rest by another sovereign decree. That terrible doctrine the Scriptures do not teach, Luther thundered; for it would make of God a terrible, arbitrary Lord who at the same time that He bespeaks mercy towards all is secretly plotting the damnation of most of mankind.

We have described herewith the substance of the controversies that racked Calvinism for years on end, down to our day. Calvin himself believed that before the fall of man into sin God had purposed the reprobation or damnation of the greater portion of mankind. This was known as supralapsarianism. Most of his followers, however, opted for a somewhat milder view, namely that after the fall it was the decision of God to pass some by, while He elected others. This was known as infralapsarianism. Today both views are largely rejected by Calvinists in favor of a kind of hypothetical universalism according to which the elect will be saved by irresistible grace and the nonelect, whom God also loves and wants to save by what is called "common grace," will be saved if they respond favorably. This is a mixture of Calvinism and synergism.

Synergism rather than Calvinism has usually been the greater threat to Lutheran churches and their followers. The Formula of Concord writers detected seeds of synergism in the writings of some Lutheran leaders of that day. Most of it was probably unintentional and would have been repudiated if its authors had been challenged. But in Melanchthon it was a considered option, for he definitely favored what might be called synergistic predestination; that God chose those in whom He foresaw a cooperating will in conversion. That can be documented from Melanchthon's writings, especially the later editions of his *Loci*. His followers tended to say the same thing. Contrariwise, there were those like Amsdorf and Brenz, who for all the world sounded like arch-Calvinists in some of their unguarded statements made in connection with man's conversion and salvation, or his unbelief and damnation.

One minor controversy among Lutherans had broken out in Strasbourg. It involved the chief pastor in the city, Marbach, and the Crypto-Calvinist professor at the university, Hieronymus Zanchi, from 1561 to 1563. Marbach stood for the historic Lutheran position, while Zanchi incorporated elements of Calvin's thought. The controversy, however, was short in duration. It was settled by the Strasbourg Formula of Concord in 1563, a document apparently written by Andreae. The role of the latter at this time may also explain in part why it was held to be imperative to include an article in the Formula of Concord. When that document appeared in 1577 Marbach in turn became one of its strongest supporters and promoters, and Zanchi openly acknowledged his pro-Calvinistic feelings.

As in all its other articles, the Formula of Concord in its 11th article (on predestination) sought to underscore the Lutheran position as taught by Luther and the Augsburg Confession. God indeed foreknows and foreordains the salvation of His elect, not willy-nilly, but through His gracious purpose wrought in the redemptory sacrifice of Christ. God's election is therefore rightly taught as a cause of man's salvation; and there is nothing in man or in his will that accounts for it. On the other hand, man's damnation is traceable alone to man's own fault, his unbelief. The reprobation that befalls certain ones is not by God's prior election, but in just recompense for their own stubborn resistance to His grace. God is not less serious, or less efficacious with them, than with those ultimately saved. There are no contradictory wills in God. It is true, however, that the antecedent will of God which earnestly seeks all, will be followed by His consequent will, if and when men reject Him in unbelief. What the Formula of Concord teaches on this subject in Article XI is in perfect agreement with its 1st and

2d article, on sin and free will, concerning man's nature and the need for God's grace unto salvation.

Synergism, it must be seen, is an effort not only to credit man with powers to cooperate in his conversion, but also an effort to locate the reason why some are saved and others not in man himself. Calvinism, while upholding the *sola gratia* teaching of Scripture, denies the universality of God's grace (contrary to hundreds of passages, including John 3:16), in an effort to show that what God intends is also that which finally happens because He is sovereign; and that thus the eventual damnation of some must be found in the eternal intent of the sovereign Lord. Lutherans, as the Formula of Concord sought to emphasize, refrain from trying to solve the mystery, especially at the expense of denying either *sola gratia* (by grace alone) or *gratia universalis* (universal grace). So, on the one hand, Lutheran theology stood back in awe before this mystery, and stated: "We should with Paul, place the finger upon our lips, remember and say, Rom. 9:20: 'O man, who art thou that repliest against God?'" On the other hand, Lutheran theology emphasized that this article, when taught in all its purity, is "a consolatory doctrine," in fact, one of God's most comforting assurances to believers who are troubled on every hand by crosses and afflictions, by onslaughts of their own flesh, the world, and Satan, and by gnawing doubts which would tear them from their Savior. To remember at such times that they who trust in Christ Jesus for the remission of all their sin are also God's very elect, whom He will not allow to be torn from His hand, is the most reassuring truth that God could speak to a troubled heart. Such are the conquerors, of whom Paul testifies with exultation in Rom. 8:28-39, to wit, that nothing shall separate them from their loving, faithful God.

# XII. Of Other Heresies and Sects

Historical Background:
SECTARIAN MOVEMENTS THAT HAD NEVER EMBRACED THE AUGSBURG CONFESSION

With the completion of Article XI the framers of the Formula of Concord were of the opinion that now "the offensive divisions that have erupted have been thoroughly adjudicated." The position in support of the Augsburg Confession on 11 controverted issues had been stated and safeguards provided against further disunity. Moreover, the scandal of disunity among Luther's followers had now ended with the prayer "that we may all be united in Him (Christ) and remain constant in such Christian unity which is pleasing to Him" (FC, Epitome, XI, 22—23).

But there still loomed the continuing threat of the sects around them. These were a motley group, often with wide differences. Sects and cults have been described as the unpaid debts of the church. That may not tell the whole story but the fact is that such fringe groups often begin and grow because of the church's failure to deal meaningfully with the proverbial "man-down-under," on the lowest rung of the social and political ladder. Only too often their "faithful" have fallen prey to radical thinking and exploitation by dynamic leaders who dangle hopes of better times, talking fast and loose of God's purported promises. Frequently this meant opposition, often violent, against the "establishment." The "established" churches—Romanist, Lutheran, and/or Calvinist—were their typical targets. They agitated for return to what they considered 1st-century Christianity, opposed existing governmental authority, and invited persecution against their extremism.

Religious radicalism was by no means a new phenomenon.

History is replete with similar earlier radical, fanatical movements. The Reformation mood simply triggered new 16th-century versions. At Wittenberg one of Luther's own colleagues, Andreas Bodenstein von Karlstadt, took advantage of Luther's forced exile at the Wartburg during the 2d half of 1521 and early 1522, to call for radical removal of every vestige of Romanist influence from the churches, including purely external decorations. The notorious Zwickau Prophets invaded the city at about the same time with their notions of direct revelations from the Spirit. "Inspired" directly by the Spirit, they refused to be held by the Biblical Word. Thomas Muenzer became the catalyst for a bloody uprising of the peasants. Many perished with him in the bloodbath at Frankenhausen.

Most notable and long-lived among the radical reform movements were the Anabaptists. The writers of the Formula of Concord recognized that the Anabaptists were "divided into many groups" and that the variety of teachings among them made it difficult to categorize them simply under one blanket description—a fact that holds true to this day. But in general, whether they were pacifist or revolutionary, they invariably caused friction or tension with existing governments, with church bodies that did not meet their supposedly early Christian standards of the truly regenerate, and, in some instances, with established mores on the home and marriage which they wanted radically transformed.

The earliest among them seemed to center in Zurich, originating from some of Zwingli's followers who considered his reform too moderate and shallow. At first they did not insist on rebaptizing but merely emphasized the need for congregations to be the gathering of the totally regenerate, measured according to their severe, legalistic notions of piety. But soon leaders like Georg Blaurock and Konrad Grebel led them to the next step, that only the genuine Christian is to be baptized. This resulted in their "rebaptizing" the "faithful," and, in turn, provided the reason why they came to be called the Anabaptists or "rebaptizers" by their opponents.

These early Anabaptists were generally pacifists. Because of their extreme views they were ruthlessly persecuted; many were killed, especially in Catholic lands or territories where their notions were judged to be a revival of the ancient Donatist heresy. Along with their rejection of infant baptism went also a general denigrating of Baptism and the Lord's Supper as vehicles of God's grace and forgiveness. They were regarded merely as symbols of conversion, and, like the Word itself, they were held to be secondary in importance to the Spirit's immediate endowment and bestowal of the "Word" directly to each true Christian member of their regenerate fellowship who yields himself to the "new" and "holy" life.

Still more radical movements sprang up elsewhere in Europe. Another notable "prophet" with a considerable following was Melchior Hoffman, who had traveled the course from Romanist to Lutheran, to Zwinglian, and finally to Anabaptist. His prophecies had an apocalyptic ring; foremost among them was his forecast that his imprisonment for 6 months would be followed by the end of the world. When that prophecy failed, his followers had some reinterpreting to do.

A much more radical group by far was that which formed around John Matthys and John of Leiden; it involved an extremely radical take-over of the whole city of Muenster in Germany's western highlands, Westphalia. Undoubtedly this abortive movement, in which John of Leiden even proclaimed himself King of the New Zion, colored most of the opposition to the Anabaptist movement in the 16th century. Existing forms of government, church, home, and family life all became targets of his fanaticism. This tragic and misguided movement ended finally after a long siege, with the recapture of the city by Catholic forces under the aegis of the ousted bishop supported by his allies.

A moderate, nonviolent direction then began among the remnants of the Anabaptist movement, led by men like Obbe Philips and Menno Simons (Mennonites). But basically many doctrinal deviations from soundly Biblical articles of faith continued. It is these which the Formula of Concord took pains to point out. Baptism remained a symbol of personal conversion which the Spirit works directly, and it must be by immersion; the Lord's Supper likewise had symbolical significance only; the Scriptures were honored but the Spirit's direct revelation to the hearts of the regenerate really stood higher; Christ's person and His work were considerably distorted and confused—not to mention also the doctrine on the Trinity—because of the emphasis on the prescribed discipline and piety of life as the basis for inclusion in the congregation of the truly regenerate; infant baptism was abjured on the ground that children of the regenerate are without sin, which meant that the doctrine of original sin was also denied. The fact that they continued to resist constituted government brought recurring pressure and civil penalties, as well as flight into more friendly territories or havens. As they went, they carried their strange "gospel" with them and their often quaint way of life and dress.

The movement led by Kaspar Schwenkfeld, while not successful and enduring of itself, was typical of another trend running parallel with the Reformation. Involved was a strange combination of "spiritualism" and "rationalism," in which the human spirit mounted in importance over the inspired Word of God. Schwenkfeld thought of his way as a kind of middle position between Romanism and Luther's theology. Actually his was a kind of extreme 16th-century "egoism." Though he had been an early supporter of Luther, by 1531 Schwenkfeld had rejected key Reformation articles like justification by faith, Scriptural authority, efficacy of the means of grace (Word and Sacrament), infant baptism, and, by his own admission, virtually all of the Augsburg Confession. Today only a few Schwenkfeldians survive, chiefly in the United States and almost exclusively in Pennsylvania.

Sebastian Franck, influenced strongly by the thinking of Erasmus, carried his humanistic distortions of the Christian faith to even greater extremes. The Spaniard Juan de Valdés, working chiefly in Italy, gathered disciples around him at Naples with similar subjectivistic and mystical sort of thinking, plus claims of direct, divine inspiration. Usually these notions were structured on strict pietism as the essence of their theology and relation with God.

These sectarian, cultic tendencies often resulted in what might be termed complete depotentiation, or stripping, of Christ's true deity and sovereign powers as the Son of God. The article on the Trinity was turned anti-Trinitarian, notably in the views of Michael Servetus, a native of Spain and a doctor. Fleeing before the Spanish Inquisition, he sought haven in Geneva. But Calvin had him burned at the stake for his heresy—an action incidentally which characterized the unfortunate severity of the Swiss Reformer's attitude against heretical teaching. Luther, on the other hand, while sharply opposing false teaching wherever he found it, never believed that the sword of the state was the answer. If the persuasive, clear Word of God could not do it, he did not believe the stake, or civil, capital punishment would accomplish a change in a heretic's thinking either.

The most enduring of the Antitrinitarian movements was

that founded by Faustus Socinus (Sozzini), who hailed from Siena, Italy. His uncle Laelius Socinus had first promoted what amounted to neo-Arian views on the doctrine of God. With their freethinking and liberal views they sought haven at first in the centers where the Reformation was breaking, believing that their frank, intellectual approach to religion would be welcome. They found, instead, that neither Wittenberg nor Geneva were open to Scripture-denying, Christ-lowering sort of theologizing. Eventually they came to Poland and were successful in gathering a considerable following, especially among the nobility. For the better part of a century they flourished. The Racovian Catechism (named after Rakow, Poland, 55 mi. northeast of Krakow) is testimony to the impact which they made there. Eventually, however, they were forced to flee from this Catholic land, seeking haven, in turn, first in Holland, then England, and eventually America, where they surfaced in the form of the Unitarian churches, having existed underground for some time in denominations like the Congregationalists and Anglicans. Inclusion in the Formula of the warning against anti-Trinitarian views warded off the encroachment of this heresy among confessionally minded Lutheran churches during succeeding centuries.

But sects and sectarianism do not give up easily. They are spawned by the same kind of subjectivism in theology that has occasioned false teaching in mainline churches, like those of Rome, Calvinism, and even Lutheranism. Whenever the Scriptural authority is set aside, the human spirit steps in. So whether from Vatican hill, or whether from the hills of Tennessee, or wherever it might be, theological meanderings have been the bane of the church's life, as the *Traumpredigten,* dream-sermons, as Luther called them, take over and shape religious life and thought. The sects are a real threat. But in spite of their egoism and aberrations, at least among them there generally is enough of the Gospel core left to call them Christian. A more dangerous threat lies in the cults— Jehovah's witnesses, Mormonism, Mary Baker Eddy's Christian Scientists, and others—where Christianity itself is blacked out. Against them the church needs eternal vigilance. The Formula of Concord's final exhortation is: "All pious Christians of high and low estate should be on guard against them, as their soul's salvation and eternal life are dear to them."

# The Formula of Concord
# Part One: The Epitome

A condensed report of the articles in controversy between the theologians of the Augsburg Confession, devoutly explained and harmonized under the guidance of God's Word in the following recapitulation.

A COMPREHENSIVE ABRIDGMENT,
RULE, AND GUIDELINE,

according to which all doctrine should be judged and the errors which have occurred explained and settled in a Christian manner.

1. We believe, teach, and confess that the only rule and guideline, according to which all doctrines and teachers alike should be judged and evaluated are solely the prophetic and apostolic Scriptures of the Old and New Testament, as it is written: "Thy Word is a lamp unto my feet and a light unto my path," Psalm 119:105. And in St. Paul: "If an angel from heaven were to come and preach differently, he shall be damned," Gal. 1:8.

Other writings, however, by old or new teachers, whatever their names, should not be held equal to the Holy Scripture. They should all be wholly subjected to the same and should not be accepted in any other manner than as witnesses of the preservation of the doctrine of the prophets and apostles in various places after the apostles' time.

2. Since false teachers and heretics crept in right after the days of the apostles, and even while they were still living, the church directed the first *symbola* against them, that is, short positive creeds, which were regarded as the unanimous, universal Christian faith and confession of the orthodox and true church, namely, the Apostles' Creed, the Nicene Creed, and the Athanasian Creed. We pledge ourselves to these and reject herewith all heresies and doctrines, which are brought into the church of God contrary to those creeds.

3. As to the polarization in matters of faith which has occurred in our time, we will hold to the same unanimous consensus and

declaration of our Christian faith and confession, especially against the papacy and its false worship, idolatry, and superstition, as well as against other sects. We will hold to the creed of our time, the original, unaltered Augsburg Confession, delivered to Charles V at Augsburg in 1530 at the great imperial diet, as well as to its Apology, and the Articles which were set forth at Smalcald in 1537 and subscribed to by the chief theologians at that time.

Since these matters also concern every layman and his soul's salvation, we acknowledge also the Small and Large Catechisms of Dr. Luther, included in his works, as the "Bible of the laity," which contain all that is more broadly treated in Holy Scripture and is necessary for a Christian to know for his salvation.

According to this guide all doctrines are to be set forth, as stated above, and whatsoever is contrary to this instruction is to be rejected and condemned as opposed to the unanimous declaration of our faith.

The distinction between the Holy Scripture, both Old Testament and New, and all other writings is retained in this manner, and the Holy Scripture remains the sole judge, norm, and guide, according to which all doctrines must be established and tested, as by the unique touchstone, whether they are good or evil, right or wrong.

But other creeds and confessions and writings previously cited are not judges like Holy Scripture, but merely witnesses and declarations of the faith, showing how at various times those who were living then understood and interpreted Holy Scripture in the disputed articles in the churches of their day, and how they rejected and condemned any teaching contrary to the Word of God.

## I. ORIGINAL SIN

The Main Question in This Dispute:

Whether original sin is to be identified without distinction with the corrupted nature, substance, and essence of man, or perhaps with the noblest and best part of his being, namely the rational soul itself in its highest state and powers; or, whether there is a difference between the substance, nature, essence, body, and soul of man also after the fall, and original sin, so that nature is one thing and original sin another, which adheres to the corrupted nature and defiles it.

## THE AFFIRMATIVE

The Pure Teaching, Faith, and Confession, Conforming to the Above Standard and Comprehensive Declaration

1. We believe, teach, and confess that a difference exists between the nature of man, not only as he was originally created by God, pure and holy, without sin, but also as we possess it now after the fall,

namely between original sin and our nature, which after the fall still is and remains a creature of God, and that this difference is as great as the difference between the work of God and the devil.

2. We believe, teach, and confess also, that this distinction is to be held with the greatest diligence. The teaching, namely, that no difference exists between our human nature and original sin, is in conflict with the chief articles of our Christian faith: creation, redemption, sanctification, and the resurrection of the flesh, and cannot be harmonized with them.

For God is not the Creator only of the body and soul of Adam and Eve before the fall, but also of our body and soul after the fall. Even though they are corrupted, God recognizes us as His creation, as it is written in Job 10:8: "Thine hands have made me and fashioned me together round about." Deut. 32:6; Is. 45:9; 54:5; 64:8; Acts 17:25-28; Ps. 100:3; 139:14; Eccl. 12:1.

Even the Son of God assumed this human nature into the unity of His person, though without sin; therefore it was not an alien flesh, but ours that He assumed, and thereby became our true brother. Heb. 2:14: "Since therefore the children share in flesh and blood, He himself likewise partook of the same nature." Again (vv. 16, 17): "He took not on Him the nature of angels, but He took on Him the seed of Abraham. Wherefore in all things it behooved Him to be made like unto His brethren," sin excepted. In like manner Christ also redeemed our human nature, which is His creation, sanctifies it as His work, raises it up from the dead as His work, and adorns it gloriously as His work. But original sin He did not create, not assume, not sanctify, neither will He raise it up with the elect, nor adorn it, nor grant it bliss—but in the resurrection it will be wholly annihilated.

The difference between the corrupted nature and the corruption, which adheres to nature and corrupts it, can here be easily recognized.

3. We believe, teach, and confess furthermore that original sin is not a slight corruption, but one so deep-seated in human nature, that nothing in the body and soul of man has remained sound or incorrupt, whether in his internal or external powers, but as the church sings:

> All mankind fell in Adam's fall,
> One common sin infects us all. [*TLH* 369:1]

This unspeakable harm cannot be recognized by reason, but only with the aid of God's Word. Nor can anyone separate such corruption from the nature of man except God alone. This will be accomplished completely through death, in the resurrection, when the nature which we now bear will rise without original sin and live eternally, wholly separated and removed from sin, as it is written in Job 19:26, 27: "I shall be clothed with this my skin and in my flesh shall I see God. I will gaze upon Him myself, and my eyes shall behold Him."

# THE NEGATIVE

Rejection of the Opposing False Teaching

1. We reject and condemn therefore the teaching that original sin is a mere debt or obligation because of another's wrongdoing, without any corruption of our own nature.

2. We likewise reject [the view] that evil inclinations are not sin, but rather an innate essential characteristic of nature, or as if the defect or damage indicated were not truly sin, for which man should be a child of wrath, separated from Christ.

3. We also reject the Pelagian error, in which it is proposed that man's nature is uncorrupted even after the fall and wholly good, especially in spiritual matters, and that it has remained pure in its *naturalibus*, i.e., in its natural powers.

4. Again, that original sin is merely a slight, negligible spot splashed on or a windblown speck, beneath which nature kept its good powers also in spiritual matters.

5. Again, that original sin is merely an external hindrance in the way of the good spiritual powers and not a despoliation or lack of them, like a magnet painted with garlic juice, by which its natural power is not removed, but merely impeded; or that this speck could easily be washed off as a spot from the face or color from the wall.

6. Again, that the human nature and essence is not wholly corrupted in man, but that man still has something good in him, also in spiritual matters, such as a capacity, an aptitude, a competence, or a power to initiate or effect something, or to cooperate in spiritual matters.

7. On the other hand, we also reject the false teaching of the Manichaeans, who teach that original sin is something essential and substantial infused into the human nature by Satan, and mixed with it, as poison and wine are mixed.

8. Again, that it is not the natural man who sins, but something other and foreign to him; and for this reason man's nature is not accused, but solely the original sin in that nature.

9. We reject and condemn as a Manichaean error also the teaching that original sin is identical with the corrupted substance and essence of man without distinction, so that after the fall no difference should be assumed to exist between nature *per se* and original sin, and that none could be discovered by reason.

10. Luther calls this original sin "natural, personal, or essential evil," not intending that "man's nature, person, or essence" is itself "original sin" without distinction, but that these words should distinguish between original sin, which has become infixed into man's nature, and the other sins, which are called actual sins.

11. For original sin is not a sin which one commits; it is a condition infixed into the nature, substance, and essence of man. Therefore, even if no evil thought should arise in the heart of

corrupted man, if no idle word were spoken, nor evil deed committed, his nature would yet be corrupted by original sin, which we inherit from sinful seed as a fountain of all actual sins, showing itself in evil thoughts, words, and deeds, as it is written: "Out of the heart proceed evil thoughts," etc. Again: "The imagination of man's heart is evil from his youth."

12. It is well to take note of the variant conceptions of the word "nature," by which the Manichaeans bemantle their error and confuse many innocent people. For at times the essence of man is meant, as when it is said: God created human nature. At times "nature" signifies the good or bad character of a thing, which inheres in its nature or essence, as when it is said: It is the serpent's nature to strike, and it is man's nature and character to sin and to be sinful. Here the word "nature" does not designate the substance of man but something which adheres to his nature or substance.

13. As to the Latin words *substantia* and *accidens*, since they are not Biblical terms, also strange to the common man, they should not be used in sermons before the general unlearned public; the simple folk should rather be spared these terms.

But in the academies and among the learned such words are rightly retained in the discussion of original sin. Here they are well known and used without any misunderstanding to designate the essence of each thing, and what is to be distinguished as an added quality.

The difference between God's work and the devil's is most clearly demonstrated in this way: The devil cannot create substance; he can only by God's permission corrupt the substance created by God in aspects not related to the substance [*per accidens*, L.].

## II. THE FREE WILL
### The State of the Controversy

The Main Question in This Dispute:

The will of man is found in four dissimilar states, namely: 1. before the fall; 2. after the fall; 3. after regeneration; 4. after the resurrection of the flesh. Here the main question concerns the will and capacity of man in the second state: What are his powers in spiritual matters after the fall of our first parents and before his regeneration? Is he able to apply himself and prepare for the grace of God by his own powers and thus accept the grace offered by the Holy Ghost in Word and holy sacraments before he is regenerated by the Spirit of God, or not?

## THE AFFIRMATIVE
The Pure Doctrine on This Article of Faith According to God's Word

1. Our teaching, faith, and confession in this matter is that man's intellect and reason is blind in spiritual matters and does not understand anything by its own powers when asked about spiritual things, as it is written, 1 Cor. 2:14: "A man who is unspiritual refuses what belongs to the Spirit of God; it is folly to him; he cannot grasp it because it needs to be judged in the light of the Spirit" [NEB].

2. Likewise we believe, teach, and confess that the unregenerate will of man is not only turned away from God but has become an enemy of God. He has an inclination and will only toward the evil and whatever is repugnant to God, as it is written: "The imagination of man's heart is evil from his youth" (Gen. 8:21). Again: "The carnal mind is enmity against God; for it is not subject to the law of God, neither, indeed, can be" (Rom. 8:7 AV). Yes, as little as a dead body can make itself alive and resume its physical earthly life, so little can a man, who is spiritually dead through sin, raise himself up to spiritual life, as it is written: "When we were dead through our trespasses, He made us alive together with Christ," Eph. 2:5 [RSV]. Therefore we also, as of ourselves, "are not capable of thinking anything good," but that we are "qualified" [NEB] is from God, 2 Cor. 3:5.

3. But God the Holy Ghost does not effect the conversion without means. Rather, He makes use of the preaching and hearing of the Word of God, as is written in Rom. 10:17: "Faith cometh by hearing of the Word of God" [AV]. It is God's will that one should hear His word and not stop one's ears (Ps. 95:8). In this Word the Holy Ghost is present and opens the hearts, so that like Lydia of Acts 16:14 they hear it and so are converted solely by the grace and power of the Holy Ghost, who alone works the conversion of men. For without grace our "wanting and running" (Rom. 9:16), our planting, sowing, and watering are all for nought, if He does not "give the increase." Thus Christ also says: "Without Me ye can do nothing" (John 15:5). With these few words He removes all powers from the free will and ascribes all to the grace of God, so that no man could boast of anything before God, 1 Cor. 9:16.

## THE NEGATIVE

The Contrary False Doctrine

Consequently we reject and condemn all the following errors as contrary to the rule of God's Word.

1. The swarm [Ger. *Schwarm*, L. *delirum*] of philosophers called Stoics, as well as the Manichaeans, who taught that all that happens must so happen, and nothing else could happen, and that man does all things by compulsion, even what he may do in external matters. He is driven to evil deeds and acts of unchastity, robbery, murder, theft, and the like.

2. We reject also the crass error of the Pelagians who taught that

man can convert himself to God by his own powers, believe the Gospel, give hearty obedience to the Law of God, and thereby earn the forgiveness of sins and eternal life without the grace of the Holy Ghost.

3. We reject also the error of the Semi-Pelagians, who teach that man can make a beginning of his conversion by his own power, but that he cannot complete it without the grace of the Holy Spirit.

4. Likewise the teaching that although man with his free will is too weak before his regeneration to make a beginning and convert himself to God by his own powers, and from the heart obey God's law; yet, when the Holy Ghost has made the beginning through the preaching of the Word and has offered grace therein, then the will of man could by his own natural powers contribute, aid, and cooperate a little in some manner, even though insignificantly and weakly, to render himself fit, to prepare himself for grace, to seize, to receive, and to believe the Gospel.

5. Again, that man after his regeneration could keep the Law of God perfectly and fulfill it completely, and that such full performance constitutes our righteousness before God, by which we merit eternal life.

6. Again, we reject and condemn the error of the enthusiasts, who imagine that God draws men to Himself, enlightens, justifies, and gives them final salvation without means, without the hearing of the Word and also without the use of the holy sacraments.

7. Again, that in conversion and regeneration God totally annihilates the substance and essence of the Old Adam and, in particular, the rational soul, and creates a new being of the soul out of nothing in the act of conversion and regeneration.

8. Again, when these ways of speaking are used without explanation: that man's will strives against the Holy Ghost before, in, and after conversion, and that the Holy Ghost is given to those who purposefully and persistently resist; for God makes willing people out of the unwilling, as Augustine says, and dwells in the willing after conversion.

Some teachers of the church, ancient and modern, have made such statements as *Deus trahit, sed volentem trahit,* that is, "God draws, but He draws the willing." Again, *Hominis voluntas in conversione non est otiosa, sed agit aliquid,* that is, "Man's will is not inactive in conversion, but also does something." Regarding such statements we hold that since they are introduced to confirm the role of the natural free will in the conversion of man, contrary to the doctrine of the grace of God, they are therefore not in harmony with the form of sound doctrine. Accordingly, it is right to avoid them when the conversion to God is under discussion.

On the other hand, it is rightly said that God in conversion makes willing men out of the obstreperously unwilling through the "drawing" of the Holy Ghost. After such conversion man's regenerated will through daily penitential practice will not be inactive, but will cooperate in all the works of the Holy Ghost, which He performs through us.

9. Again, when Luther wrote that man's will remains "purely passive" [Weimar ed., 18, 697], that is, he does nothing at all, this is to be understood *respectu divinae gratiae in accendendis novis motibus,* that is, the Spirit of God seizes man's will in the hearing of the Word or the use of the holy sacraments and brings about the new birth and conversion. When the Holy Ghost has effected and completed this, and man's will is changed and renewed "solely through His divine power," then the new will of man is an instrument and tool of God, the Holy Spirit, so that he not only accepts grace but also cooperates in subsequent works of the Holy Ghost.

Thus, before the conversion of man only two effective means are present, namely, the Holy Ghost and the Word of God as the instrument of the Holy Ghost, by which He effects the conversion. It is intended that man should hear the Word, but he cannot by his own powers obtain faith. Only by the grace and working of God the Holy Ghost can he receive it.

## III. THE RIGHTEOUSNESS OF FAITH BEFORE GOD
### The State of the Controversy

**The Main Question in This Dispute:**

While it is unanimously confessed in our churches in accordance with God's Word and the content of the Augsburg Confession, that we poor sinners are justified before God and saved solely through faith in Christ, and thus Christ alone is our righteousness, who is true God and man, because in Him the divine and human natures are united in one person (Jer. 23:6; 1 Cor. 1:30; 2 Cor. 5:21), a question has been raised: According to which nature is Christ our righteousness? Two contradictory errors have broken out in several churches.

One faction has held that Christ is our righteousness only according to the divine nature, whereby He dwells in us by faith. In contrast to the Godhead, which dwells in us by faith, all human sin is regarded as a drop of water over against the great ocean. Contrary to this, others have held that Christ is our righteousness before God only according to the human nature.

### THE AFFIRMATIVE

The Pure Doctrine of the Christian Churches Against Both Errors Here Set Forth

1. Against both of these errors just named, we unanimously

believe, teach, and confess that Christ is our righteousness neither according to the divine nature alone, nor according to the human nature alone, but that the whole Christ according to both natures is our righteousness. Alone by His obedience, which He rendered to the Father unto death as God and man, did He merit forgiveness of sins and eternal life for us, as it is written: "For as through the obedience of the one man the many will be made righteous," Rom. 5:19 [NEB].

2. Therefore we believe, teach, and confess, that our righteousness before God is this: God forgives our sin purely by grace, without any preceding, accompanying, or subsequent works, merit, or worthiness. He grants and imputes to us the righteousness of the obedience of Christ, and on account of this righteousness we are accepted into grace by God and are accounted righteous.

3. We believe, teach, and confess that faith alone is the means and instrument, by which we make Christ ours, and thereby in Christ also that "righteousness which is valid before God," on whose account such "faith is accounted unto us for righteousness," Rom. 4:5 [AV].

4. We believe, teach, and confess that this faith is not a mere knowledge of the stories about Christ, but such a gift of God by which we rightly come to know Christ, our Redeemer, in the Word of the Gospel and trust in Him, so that we have forgiveness of sins by grace, alone on account of His obedience, and are accounted holy and righteous before God the Father and have eternal salvation.

5. We believe, teach, and confess, that according to the usage of Scripture the word "justify" in this article means "to absolve," that is, declare free from sin. Prov. 17:15: "He that justifieth the wicked, and he that condemneth the righteous, even they both are abomination to the Lord." Also Rom. 8:33: "Who shall lay anything to the charge of God's elect? It is God that justifieth."

If in its stead the words *regeneratio* and *vivificatio* are used, that is, "rebirth" and "making alive," as is done in the Apology, it is done in the same sense in which the renewal of man is understood otherwise. These are rightly [L. *recte*] distinguished from the justification by faith.

6. We believe, teach, and confess also, even though much weakness and frailty still clings to those rightly believing and truly regenerate, even to the grave, that nevertheless they have no cause to doubt either their righteousness, which is accorded them through faith, nor their soul's salvation, but hold fast to the certainty that on account of Christ they have a gracious God in accordance with the promise and Word of the Holy Gospel.

7. We believe, teach, and confess that for the maintenance of the pure doctrine concerning the righteousness of faith before God special diligence should be given to the *particulis exclusivis* ([exclusive particles, or] words of exclusion), that is, to the following words of the holy Apostle Paul, by which the merit of Christ is kept wholly apart from our works, and the glory is given to Christ alone.

The holy Apostle Paul writes: "By grace," "without merit," "without the Law," "without works," "not of works," etc. (Eph. 2:8; Rom. 1:17; 3:24; 4:3 ff.; Gal. 3:11; Heb. 11). These words altogether declare that we are justified and saved "alone through faith" in Christ.

8. We believe, teach, and confess that although the contrition preceding and the good works following do not belong to the article of justification before God, nevertheless no such faith should be imagined, which could be and abide together with the evil intention to sin and act against one's conscience. Rather, after a man has been justified by faith, then there is a true, living "faith which worketh by love" (Gal. 5:6 [AV]). Thus good works always follow after justifying faith, and if faith is upright, they will certainly be found together with it, for faith is never alone, but is always accompanied by love and hope.

## THE NEGATIVE

The Opposing Doctrine Rejected

We therefore reject and condemn all the following errors:

1. That Christ is our righteousness only according to the divine nature, etc.

2. That Christ is our righteousness only according to the human nature, etc.

3. That in the statements of the prophets and apostles regarding "the righteousness of faith" and "being justified" they do not mean "absolving" or "being absolved from sins," but that on the contrary they mean being made righteous before God on account of and through the love and virtue poured into man by the Holy Ghost and the works and deeds which follow.

4. That faith does not look only upon the obedience of Christ, but upon His divine nature as it dwells and works in us, and how through such indwelling our sins are covered.

5. That faith is such a trust in the obedience of Christ, that it could be and remain in a man, even if he has no true repentance, and no love flows from it, but who rather abides in sins against his conscience.

6. That not God Himself but only His gifts dwell in the believers.

7. That faith confers salvation because the renewal, consisting of love toward God and the neighbor, was initiated by faith.

8. That faith has the preeminence in justification, nevertheless the renewal and love also belong to our righteousness before God in such a manner, that even though it is not the principle cause of our righteousness, yet without this love and renewal our righteousness before God would not be whole or perfect.

9. That the believers are justified before God and saved at the same time through the imputed righteousness of Christ and also through the beginning of the new obedience, or, in part through the

imputed righteousness of Christ, and in part through the beginning of the new obedience.

10. That the promise of grace becomes ours through the faith in the heart and through the confession made with the mouth, as well as through other virtues.

11. That faith does not justify without good works, with the result that good works are of necessity required for righteousness, and that without their presence man could not be justified.

## IV. GOOD WORKS
## The State of the Controversy

### The Main Question in the Dispute About Good Works

Two disagreements arose in several churches concerning the doctrine of good works:

1. In the first instance several theologians were divided over the following assertions, in which one group wrote: Good works are necessary for salvation; it is impossible to be saved without good works. Again: No man was ever saved without good works.

Contrary to this, the other group wrote: Good works are injurious to salvation.

2. Thereupon a conflict arose between some theologians concerning the two words "necessary" and "free," in which one side contended that the word "necessary" is not to be used with regard to the new obedience, which flows not from necessity and compulsion, but from the free and willing spirit. The other side insisted upon the word "necessary," because this obedience is not a matter of our choice, but regenerated people are obligated to render such obedience.

From this disputation concerning the words there developed a controversy on the matter itself, in which one side contended that the law should not at all be cultivated among Christians, but that people should be admonished to good works solely from the Gospel. The other side contradicted this.

## THE AFFIRMATIVE
Pure Doctrine of the Christian Churches in This Controversy

In a thorough explanation of this controversy and its adjudication this is our teaching, faith, and confession:

1. That good works will surely and without doubt follow after the true faith as the fruits of a good tree, if that faith is not dead, but living.

2. We believe, teach, and confess also that good works are to be wholly excluded, both in the question of salvation and in the article of

justification before God, as the apostle testified in clear words, when he wrote: "In the same sense David speaks of the happiness of the man whom God accounts as just, apart from any specific acts of righteousness: 'Happy are they,' he says, whose lawless deeds are forgiven, whose sins are buried away,' " Rom. 4:6-8 [NEB]. And again: "For it is by His grace you are saved, through trusting in Him; it is not your own doing. It is God's gift, not a reward for work done. There is nothing for anyone to boast of," Eph. 2:8-9.

3. We believe, teach, and confess also, that all men, especially those regenerated and renewed through the Holy Ghost, are under obligation to do good works.

4. In this sense the words "necessary," "should," and "must" are used in a proper and Christian manner regarding the regenerate and are by no means contrary to the pattern of sound words and statements.

5. Yet the words mentioned, "necessity," and "necessary" are not to be understood as coercion, when the regenerate are under consideration, but only as the obedience due, which true believers, since they are regenerate, render not by coercion or the compulsion of the law, but of a free and willing spirit, because they are "no longer under the law, but under grace" (Rom. 6:14; 7:6; 8:14).

6. Accordingly we believe, teach, and confess also, when it is said: The regenerate do good works from a free spirit—that this is not to be understood, as if the regenerate man had the option to do good or to refrain, as he pleases, and still keep the faith, even if he perseveres in sin by design.

7. This is not to be understood otherwise than the Lord Christ explained (Rom. 8:15), namely that the liberated spirit acts thus, not out of fear of punishment as a slave, but as a child, out of love for righteousness.

8. Nevertheless, this willingness of the elect children of God is not perfect; they are still burdened with great weakness, as St. Paul complains regarding himself, Rom. 7:14 f.; Gal. 5:17.

9. This weakness is however not reckoned against the elect, on account of the Lord Christ, as it is written: "There is no condemnation for those who are united with Christ Jesus," Rom. 8:1.

10. We believe, teach, and confess also, that works do not maintain the faith and salvation in us, but the spirit of God alone, through faith, of whose presence and indwelling the good works give witness.

## THE NEGATIVE

The False Contrary Doctrine

1. Therefore we reject and condemn the manner of speaking, when it is taught and written, that good works are necessary for salvation. Again, that no man was ever saved without good works. Again, that it is impossible to be saved without good works.

2. We reject and condemn also this bare statement as offensive and harmful to Christian discipline, when it is said: Good works are detrimental to salvation.

For it is not less necessary, especially in these last times, to exhort people to Christian discipline and good works, and to remind them how necessary it is, that they exercise themselves in good works as a demonstration of their faith and gratitude toward God, than to refrain from mingling works in the articles of justification. People can be damned by an Epicurean delusion regarding faith as well as through the papistic and Pharisaic confidence in their own works and merit.

3. We condemn and reject also the teaching that faith and the indwelling of the Holy Ghost cannot be lost by willful sinning, but the saints and elect retain the Holy Spirit, even if they fall into adultery and other sins and persevere therein.

## V. LAW AND GOSPEL
The State of the Controversy

The Principal Question in This Dispute:

Whether the proper preaching of the Gospel is not only a preaching of grace, which proclaims the forgiveness of sins, but also a preaching of repentance and punishment, which chastises the unbelief, not rebuked in the Law, but only in the Gospel.

### THE AFFIRMATIVE
The Pure Teaching of God's Word

1. We believe, teach, and confess, that the difference between Law and Gospel is to be observed with great diligence in the churches as a particularly glorious light, by which the Word of God is rightly divided according to the admonition of St. Paul.

2. We believe, teach, and confess, that the Law is properly a divine teaching, which sets forth what is right and pleasing to God, and rebukes all that is sin and contrary to the will of God.

3. Therefore everything that rebukes sin is and belongs to the preaching of the Law.

4. The Gospel is properly a doctrine that teaches what a man who has not kept the law and is damned by it should believe, namely that Christ has expiated and paid for all sin, and that, without any merit on the part of man, Christ has obtained and earned forgiveness for him, "the righteousness of God," and eternal life, Rom. 1:17.

5. Since, however, the word "Gospel" is not used in only one sense in Holy Scripture, whereby this dissension originally arose, we believe, teach, and confess, that by the word "Gospel" the entire

doctrine of Christ is understood, which He, and the apostles also, professed in His teaching ministry. (In this sense it is used in Mark 1:15; Acts 20:24.) It is therefore proper to say and write that the Gospel is a proclamation of repentance and forgiveness of sins.

6. But when the Law and Gospel are held in contrast to each other, so that Moses is regarded as a teacher of the Law and Christ a preacher of the Gospel, we believe, teach, and confess, that the Gospel is not a preaching of repentance and punishment, but properly nothing other than a preaching of comfort and a joyous message that neither punishes nor terrifies but rather comforts consciences against the terror of the Law. It points only to the merit of Christ and raises up consciences with the delightful proclamation of the grace and favor of God, attained through the merit of Christ.

7. As to the revelation of sin—while the veil of Moses hangs before the eyes of all men, as long as they hear solely the preaching of the Law and nothing about Christ, they do not properly learn to recognize their sin from the Law. They either become brazen hypocrites as the Pharisees, or despair, as Judas did, etc. Therefore Christ takes the Law in His hand and explains it spiritually, Matt. 5:21-48; Rom. 7:14. Thus God's wrath is revealed from heaven upon all sinners in its true magnitude. By this they are directed to the law, from which they now truly learn to know their sin. Moses could never have brought about such understanding by force.

Accordingly, though the preaching of the suffering and death of Christ, the Son of God, is a severe and terrifying proclamation and a sign of God's wrath, by which alone mankind is properly introduced to the Law, after the veil of Moses has been put aside, so that they truly recognize, what great things God demands of us in the Law, none of which we can perform, with the result that we should seek all our righteousness in Christ:

8. Yet as long as all this, namely, Christ's suffering and death, preaches God's wrath and terrifies man, it is not properly the preaching of the Gospel but the proclamation of Moses and the Law. It is still a work foreign to Christ, through which He arrives at His own peculiar office, that is, to preach grace, to comfort, and to make alive, which alone is the real message of the Gospel.

## THE NEGATIVE

The Contrary Doctrine, Which Is Rejected

Therefore we reject and count it as false and harmful when it is taught that the Gospel is in part a preaching of repentance and punishment, and not of grace alone. By this the Gospel is again transformed into a legal doctrine; the merit of Christ and the Holy Scripture are obscured, Christians are robbed of true comfort, and the doors are again opened for the papacy.

## VI. THE THIRD USE OF THE LAW
## The State of the Controversy

### The Principal Question in This Debate

The law was given to mankind for a threefold reason: 1. that thereby an outward discipline should be maintained against wild, disobedient people; 2. that by it man might be led to the acknowledgment of his sins; 3. that they might have a sure guide, according to which they should order and govern their whole lives after they are regenerated, because the flesh still adheres to them. A division arose between several theologians concerning the 3d use of the law, namely, whether the same use of the law is to be urged among regenerate Christians, or not? One side said yes, the other no.

## THE AFFIRMATIVE

### The True Doctrine in This Controversy

1. We believe, teach, and confess that although those who truly believe, who are genuinely converted to God, are freed through Christ and delivered from the curse and compulsion of the law, yet they are not without the Law for that reason, but are rather redeemed by the Son of God for the purpose, that they might exercise themselves therein day and night, Ps. 119:1. For our first parents likewise did not live without the Law before the fall, for the law of God was written into their hearts, inasmuch as they had been created in the image of God.

2. We believe, teach, and confess that the preaching of the Law is not to be carried on only among the unbelievers and the unrepentant, but also with diligence among the truly believing, the genuinely converted, the regenerate, and those justified by faith.

3. For although they are regenerated and renewed in the spirit of their mind, such regeneration and renewal is not yet complete in this world, but only begun. In the spirit of their minds the believers are engaged in a constant battle against the flesh, that is, against the corrupted nature and manner, which adheres to us unto death. On account of the Old Adam, who still abides in the understanding, will, and all powers of man, it is necessary that the law of God should always light their way before them, lest they undertake to devise arbitrary forms of worship in self-willed human devotion. Likewise, the Old Adam should not be given his own will, but rather contrary to his will, he should be compelled not only by admonition and the threat of the Law, but even by punishments and torments, that he may submit to the Spirit and render himself captive, 1 Cor. 9:27; Rom. 6:12; Gal. 6:14; Ps. 119:1; Heb. 13:21.

4. As to the difference between the works of the Law and the fruits of the Spirit, we believe, teach, and confess that the works which are

done under the Law, are and must be called works of the Law as long as they are forced from men solely by the application of the punishments and the threat of God's wrath.

5. Fruits of the Spirit, however, are the works that the Holy Spirit, who dwells in the believers, effects through the regenerate and that are done by the believers, inasmuch as they are reborn, as if they knew of no command, threat, or reward. In this manner, then, the children of God live in the Law and walk according to the law of God. This way of life St. Paul in his epistles calls "the law of Christ" and "the law of the mind," also being "not under the Law, but under grace." Rom. 6:14; Rom. 7:23; 8:1, 14;

6. Thus the Law is and remains the same, both for the penitent and impenitent, for the regenerate and unregenerate, namely, the unalterable will of God. The difference, where obedience is concerned, is found in men, among whom the one, who is not yet regenerate, does what is required by the Law out of compulsion and unwillingly, even as the regenerate does what is demanded of him according to the flesh. But the believer does without compulsion and with a willing spirit, what no threat of the Law could ever extort from him, because he is born again.

## THE NEGATIVE
### The Contrary False Doctrine

Accordingly we reject as a harmful doctrine and error, adverse to Christian discipline and true piety, when it is taught that the Law is not to be urged in the above manner and measure among the Christians and true believers, but only among the unbelievers, non-Christians, and unrepentant.

## VII. HOLY COMMUNION

Although the Zwinglian teachers are not to be counted among the theologians relating to the Augsburg Confession, since they withdrew immediately from this confession when it was delivered, nevertheless we have desired to add a needed report on this controversy, since they try to infiltrate and spread their error under the guise of the Christian confession named above.

### The State of the Controversy

The Chief Controversy Between Us and the Sacramentarians' Doctrine in This Article:

Are the true body and blood of our Lord Jesus Christ truly and essentially present in the Holy Supper? Are they distributed with the bread and wine and received with the mouth by all who use this sacrament, be they worthy or unworthy, pious or impious, believing or unbelieving? Is it for the believers unto comfort and life, for the unbelievers unto judgment?

The Sacramentarians say no; we say yes.

To explain this controversy it is to be observed first, that there are two kinds of Sacramentarians. Some are gross Sacramentarians, who assert in emphatic, clear words what they believe in their hearts: that in the Holy Supper nothing but bread and wine are present, distributed, and received with the mouth. Others, again, are deceptive and the very worst Sacramentarians, who in part appear to speak wholly with our words and assert that they also believe in a true presence of the very, essential, living body and blood of Christ in Holy Communion, but that this takes place spiritually, through faith. But these maintain their first gross opinion under the above glowing words, namely, that nothing but bread and wine are present in the Holy Communion, and are received by mouth.

"Spiritual" means nothing more to them than the presence of the spirit of Christ or the power of the absent body of Christ and His merit, but that the body of Christ is present in no way or manner, but only above in the highest heaven, to which we lift ourselves in the thoughts of our faith and should seek His body and blood, but not at all in the bread and wine of Communion.

## THE AFFIRMATIVE

The Confession of the Pure Doctrine of Holy Communion Against the Sacramentarians

1. We believe, teach, and confess that the body and blood of Christ are truly and essentially present and are truly distributed and received with the bread and wine in Holy Communion.

2. We believe, teach, and confess that the words of Christ's testament are not to be understood differently than they read according to the letter, so that bread does not mean the absent body of Christ, nor wine the absent blood of Christ, but that it is truly the body and blood of Christ because of the sacramental union.

3. As to the consecration, we believe, teach, and confess that it is not man's work which effects such a presence of the body and blood of Christ in Holy Communion, nor the speaking of the minister, but that this is solely and alone to be ascribed to the almighty power of our Lord Jesus Christ.

4. In addition, however, we believe, teach, and confess unanimously that in the use of Holy Communion the words of institution are by no means to be omitted, but are to be publicly spoken, as it is written: "The cup of blessing, which we bless," etc. 1 Cor. 11:23-25. This blessing is accomplished through speaking the words of Christ.

5. The foundations upon which we stand in this matter against the Sacramentarians, are, as Dr. Luther has stated in his Large Confession:

"The first is this article of our Christian faith: Jesus Christ is true, essential, natural, perfect God and man in one person, inseparable and undivided."

"The second: God's right hand is everywhere, at which Christ is seated in deed and truth according to the human nature, where neither man nor angel are seated, except the Son of Mary alone, wherefore He is capable of these things, and presently reigns and has all things that are in heaven and earth in His hands and under His feet."

"The third: God's Word is not false or untruthful."

"The fourth: God has and knows various ways, in which He can be present at a place, and not only the one way, which the philosophers call 'spatial.'"

6. We believe, teach, and confess that the body and blood of Christ are received with the bread and wine on account of the sacramental union, not only spiritually by faith, but also orally, as the words of Christ clearly testify—though not in a Capernaitic, but in a supernatural, heavenly manner. Christ commands us to take, eat, and drink, as the apostles did; for it is written, "And they all drank of it," Mark 14:23. St. Paul likewise says: "The bread, which we break, is it not the Communion of the body of Christ," that is: whoever eats this bread eats the body of Christ. This is witnessed to unanimously also by the chief ancient church fathers, Chrysostom, Cyprian, Leo I, Gregory, Ambrose, Augustine, etc.

7. We believe, teach, and confess that not only the true believers and the worthy, but also the unworthy and unbelievers, receive the true body and blood of Christ, though not for life and comfort, but for judgment and damnation, if they are not converted and repentant.

For although they drive Christ from themselves as Redeemer, they are compelled to admit Him again as severe Judge. He will be as present in the judgment, which He exercises and demonstrates in the unrepentant guests, as He is now, while He offers life and comfort to the hearts of truly believing and worthy guests.

8. We believe, teach, and confess that there is only one kind of unworthy guest, namely those who do not believe, of whom it is written: "He that believeth not is judged already" (John 3:18). This judgment is aggravated by the unworthy use of the Holy Sacrament and becomes greater and heavier. 1 Cor. 11:27, 29.

9. We believe, teach, and confess that no true believer receives Holy Communion to his judgment as long as he keeps the living faith, however weak it might be. The Lord's Supper was instituted especially for the weak but penitent Christians for a comfort and strengthening of their weak faith.

10. We believe, teach, and confess that all worthiness of the guests

at this heavenly banquet consists solely in the most holy obedience and perfect merit of Christ, which we make our own through true faith, and of which we are made certain through the sacrament—but not at all through our virtues, our internal and external preparations.

## THE NEGATIVE

The Contrary and Condemned Doctrines of the Sacramentarians

Against this we unanimously reject and condemn all the following erroneous articles, which are opposed and contrary to a simple faith and confession regarding Christ's Last Supper, here stated:

1. The papistic transubstantiation, according to which it is taught in the papacy, that bread and wine lose their substance and natural essence in Holy Communion and are thus annihilated, so that they are transmuted into the body of Christ, and that only the external form remains.

2. The papistic sacrificial mass for the sins of the living and the dead.

3. That only one element of the sacrament is offered to the laity, and that contrary to the explicit word of the testament of Christ the cup is withheld from them and they are robbed of His blood.

4. When it is taught that the words of the testament of Christ are not to be understood and believed in a simple sense, as they read, but that they are dark sayings, whose understanding must first be sought in other passages.

5. That the body of Christ is not received with the mouth in the Holy Sacrament together with the bread, but that the bread and wine are received only by mouth, while the body of Christ is received only spiritually by faith.

6. That bread and wine are mere marks of recognition in the Holy Supper by which Christians mutually acknowledge one another.

7. That bread and wine are merely figures, similitudes, and types of the most distantly remote body and blood of Christ.

8. That bread and wine are mere aids to the memory, a seal and pledge, by which we are assured, that when faith will soar heavenward, it will as truly receive the body and blood of Christ there as it truly ate and drank bread and wine in Communion.

9. That our faith is made secure and confirmed in Holy Communion by the outward signs of bread and wine, and not through the body and blood of Christ, which are truly present.

10. That in the Lord's Supper only the power, the operation, and the merit of the absent body and blood of Christ are distributed.

11. That the body of Christ is enclosed in heaven in such a manner, that it can in no wise at one time be present in many or all places on earth, where His Holy Supper is celebrated.

12. That Christ could not have promised nor delivered the

essential presence of His body and blood in Holy Communion because the nature and attributes of His adopted human nature could neither bear nor allow it.

13. That God in all His omnipotence is not able (what blasphemy this is!) to bring it about that His body can be present in essence in more than one place at one time.

14. That it is not the omnipotent Word of the testament of Christ, but faith, which creates and causes the presence of the body and blood of Christ in Holy Communion.

15. That the believers should not seek the body of Christ in the bread and wine of the Holy Supper, but should lift up their eyes from the bread heavenward, and there seek the body of Christ.

16. That the unbelieving, impenitent Christians do not receive the true body and blood of Christ in Holy Communion, but only the bread and wine.

17. That the unworthiness of the guests at this heavenly banquet rests not only upon the true faith in Christ, but also upon man's external preparation.

18. That also the true believers who have and keep a true, living, pure faith in Christ can receive this sacrament unto judgment, because they are still imperfect in their outward conduct.

19. That the external, visible elements, bread and wine, should be adored in the Holy Sacrament.

20. In like manner we commit to the righteous judgment of God all idle, mocking, blasphemous questions and expressions (not repeated here for decency's sake), which are offered in a coarse, carnal, Capernaitic, and abominable manner regarding the supernatural, heavenly mysteries of this sacrament by the Sacramentarians in an altogether blasphemous manner, and with great offense [to the church, L.].

21. We also totally condemn hereby the Capernaitic eating of the body of Christ, as when one tears his flesh with his teeth and digests it as other food. The Sacramentarians maliciously charge this against us, contrary to the testimony of their own conscience and despite our abundant testimony. Hereby they make our doctrine hated among their hearers.

On the basis of the simple words of the testament of Christ we believe in a true, but supernatural, eating of the body of Christ and drinking of His blood—which human senses and reason cannot comprehend. But we have taken our reason captive to obey Christ, as in all articles of faith. Such mystery is revealed only in the Word and comprehended solely by faith.

## VIII. THE PERSON OF CHRIST

Out of the controversy on Holy Communion there developed a disunity between the genuine theologians of the Augsburg Confession and the Calvinists (who confused certain other theologians also) regarding the person of Christ, the two natures, and their attributes.

## The State of the Controversy
### The Chief Conflict in This Dissension:

The principal question was, whether the divine and human natures *realiter*, that is, in deed and truth, have a mutual sharing with each other for the sake of the personal union, sharing also the attributes of each in the person of Christ, and how far this sharing extends.

The Sacramentarians have maintained that the divine and human natures are personally united in Christ in such a manner, that neither *realiter*, that is, in deed and truth, shares with the other what is characteristic of each nature, but that they have only the name in common. They declare plainly that "the names used in common establish the union," that is, that the personal union makes only the names common. Thus, namely, God is called man, and man God, but in such a manner, that God has nothing *realiter*, i.e., in deed and truth, in common with the human nature, and the human nature has nothing in common with divinity, its majesty and its attributes. Dr. Luther and those supporting him held the opposite viewpoint against the Sacramentarians.

## THE AFFIRMATIVE
### The Pure Doctrine of the Christian Churches Regarding the Person of Christ

To explain this controversy and to decide it in accordance with our Christian faith, our doctrine, faith, and confession is as follows:

1. That the divine and human natures are personally united in Christ, so that there are not two Christs, one the Son of God, the other the Son of man, Luke 1:31-35; Rom. 9:5.

2. We believe, teach, and confess that the divine and human natures are not compounded into one substance; neither is changed into the other, but each retains its essential properties, which by no means become the properties of the other nature.

3. The properties of the divine nature are: almighty, eternal, infinite, existing by itself according to the attributes of its nature and its natural essence, omnipresent, omniscient, etc., which can never become the properties of the human nature.

4. The properties of the human nature are: being a physical creature, consisting of flesh and blood, finite and circumscribed, to suffer, to die, to ascend and descend, to move from place to place, to suffer hunger, thirst, cold, heat, and the like, which never become the properties of the divine nature.

5. Since both natures are united personally, that is, into one person, we believe, teach, and confess that this union is not such a joining or combination, that neither nature has anything personally in common with the other, that is, because of the personal union, as if one laminated two boards together, where neither gives anything to the other, nor receives from the other. Here is, rather, the very highest communion which God has with man. From this personal union and the resulting exalted and inexpressible communion there flows everything human, that is said and believed about God, and everything divine, that is said and believed about the man, Christ. The ancient church fathers explained this union and communion of natures by the comparison with glowing iron and the union of body and soul in man.

6. Therefore we believe, teach, and confess that God is man and man God, which could not be if the divine and human natures had no communion at all with each other in deed and in truth.

For how could the man, Mary's son, truly be called, or be God, or the Son of the Highest, if his humanity were not personally united with the Son of God and thus *realiter,* i.e., in deed and truth? He would have nothing but the name of God in common with Him.

7. Therefore we believe, teach, and confess that Mary conceived and bore not a mere man, pure and simple, but the very Son of God. Therefore she is rightly called, and truly is, the mother of God.

8. Therefore we believe, teach, and confess also that it was not a man, pure and simple, who suffered for us, died, was buried, descended into hell, rose from the dead, ascended into heaven, and is seated in the majesty and almighty power of God for us—but such a man, whose human nature has such deep and inexpressible union and communion with the Son of God, that it is one person with Him.

9. Therefore the Son of God has truly suffered for us, but in the attribute of the human nature, which He assumed into oneness with His divine person, and made it His own, in order that He could suffer and be our high priest for our reconciliation with God, as it is written: They have "crucified the Lord of glory," and "We are purchased with God's own blood," 1 Cor. 2:8; Acts 20:28.

10. Therefore we believe, teach, and confess that the Son of man is exalted *realiter,* i.e., in deed and truth, to the right hand of God according to the human nature, because this man [L.] was assumed into God when he was conceived in the womb by the Holy Ghost, and his human nature was personally united with the Son of the Highest.

11. This majesty He always possessed because of the personal union, though in the state of humiliation He did without it, and for that reason truly increased in age, wisdom, and favor with God and man. Therefore He did not show His majesty at all times, but when it pleased Him, until He fully laid aside the form of a servant, though not the human nature, after His resurrection, and was established in the full use, revelation, and demonstration of His divine majesty, and

thus entered into His glory. Now it is not only as God, but also as man that He knows all things, has all power, is present with all creatures, and everything in heaven, on earth, and under the earth is under His feet and in His hands (John 13:3), as He Himself testifies: "All power is given unto Me in heaven and in earth." And St. Paul: "He ascended up far above all heavens, that He might fill all things." Eph. 4:10. This His power He can exercise everywhere in His omnipresence, and all things are possible to Him, and all things known.

12. Therefore He is able, and for Him it is an easy thing, since He is present, to share His true body and blood in Holy Communion, *not according to the manner or attribute of the human nature, but according to the mode and attribute of God's right hand*, as Dr. Luther expresses our Christian childlike faith [L.: as Luther is accustomed to say according to the analogy of our Christian faith comprehended in catechesis]. This presence is not physical, nor Capernaitic, though true and essential, as the words of His testament declare: "This is, is, is my body," etc. (Luther). Matt. 26:26; Mark 14:22; Luke 22:19; 1 Cor. 11:24.

Through this our doctrine, faith, and confession the person of Christ is not divided, as Nestorius did. He denied the communication of attributes, i.e., the true sharing of the properties of both natures in Christ, and thus divided the person, as Luther declares in the book on the councils. Neither does our pious doctrine [L.] fuse the natures with their attributes into one essence, as Eutyches mistakenly did. Nor is the human nature in the person of Christ denied or abolished. Again, neither nature is changed into the other, but Christ is and remains God and man in all eternity in one undivided person. This is the greatest mystery after the Holy Trinity, as the apostle testifies (1 Tim. 3:16), on which alone rests all [L.] our comfort, life, and blessedness.

## THE NEGATIVE

The Contrary False Doctrine Concerning the Person of Christ

We therefore reject and condemn as contrary to God's Word and our simple Christian faith all the following erroneous articles, which teach:

1. That God and man are not one person in Christ, but that one person is the Son of God and the other the Son of man, as Nestorius foolishly held.

2. That the divine and human natures were compounded into one essence, and that the human nature was changed into the deity, as Eutyches fanatically held.

3. That Christ is not true, natural, eternal God, as Arius blasphemously [L.] held.

4. That Christ did not possess a true human nature with body and soul, as Marcion imagined.

5. That the personal union causes only the names and titles to be held in common.

6. That it is merely a cliche and *modus loquendi,* i.e., a manner of speaking, when it is said: God is man, man is God; for in fact, *realiter,* divinity has nothing in common with humanity, as also humanity has nothing in common with divinity.

7. That it is mere verbal communication without substance [L.], i.e., nothing but words, when it is said that the Son of God died for the sin of the world, or that the Son of man has become almighty.

8. That the human nature in Christ has become an infinite being like the Godhead in this manner, that from the essential, imparted power and quality, infused into the human nature and separated from God, the divine nature in Christ is present everywhere.

9. That the human nature in Christ has been made equal to and has become like the divine nature in its substance and being, that is, in its essential attributes.

10. That the human nature of Christ has been stretched in space to all places in heaven and earth, a matter not even attributed to the divine nature.

11. That it is impossible for Christ to be in more than one place at one time because of the attributes of the human nature, much less to be omnipresent according to the body.

12. That only the bare humanity suffered for us and redeemed us, and that the Son of God had no share in the suffering with the human nature in this function, as if it did not concern Him.

13. That Christ is present among us on earth in all our tribulations by Word and Sacrament only according to His Godhead, and that this presence has nothing at all to do with the human nature, according to which He has nothing more to do with us on earth after He redeemed us through His suffering and death.

14. That the Son of God, who assumed the human nature, does not perform all the works of His omnipotence in, by, and with the human nature after He laid aside the form of a servant, but only some of His works, and those only in the place where His human nature is locally present.

15. That according to the human nature He is not at all the possessor of omnipotence and other attributes of the divine nature, is contrary to the express statement of Christ: "All power is given unto Me in heaven and in earth"; and of St. Paul: "In Him dwelleth all the fulness of the Godhead bodily" (Matt. 28:18; Col. 2:9).

16. That greater power is given to Him in heaven and earth, namely, greater and more than to all angels and other creatures, but that He has no share in the omnipotence of God, neither was it given to Him. Thus they invent a mediocre power, i.e., a power between the omnipotence of God and the power of other creatures, and this, they hold, was given to Christ according to His human nature after His

exaltation, less than divine omnipotence, but greater than the power of other creatures.

17. That according to His human spirit there is a certain limit upon Christ, how much He ought to know, and that He shall not know more than is proper and necessary for His office as judge.

18. That Christ does not yet possess the perfect knowledge of God, though it is written of Him that in Him "are hid all the treasures of wisdom and knowledge," Col. 2:3.

19. That it is impossible for Christ to know according to His human spirit that which was from eternity, what is happening everywhere today, and what is still to come in eternity.

20. We reject and condemn also [L.] the teaching (and the passage, Matt. 28:18: "All power is given unto Me," etc. is interpreted and blasphemously distorted, so that Christ was restored to the divine nature in His resurrection and ascension), that all power in heaven and earth were restored to Him, as if in the humiliation He had laid aside and relinquished such powers according to the divine nature.

Not only are the words of Christ's testament perverted by this doctrine, but the way is also prepared for the condemned Arian heresy, so that finally Christ is denied the eternal Godhead. If such false doctrine is not contradicted on the solid foundation of God's Word and our simple Christian creed, Christ will be lost altogether, along with our salvation.

# IX. THE DESCENT INTO HELL
## The State of the Controversy

### The Chief Dispute Concerning This Article:

There has been controversy on this article also among some theologians adhering to the Augsburg Confession, namely when and in what manner the Lord Christ descended into hell according to our simple Christian creed, whether it took place before or after his death; or, whether it was done by the soul alone, or by the Godhead alone, or by body and soul; also, whether this article belongs to the suffering or to Christ's glorious victory and triumph.

But since this article, as also the preceding, cannot be comprehended by the senses nor by reason, but must be accepted solely by faith, it is our unanimous opinion that this should not be debated, but rather taught and believed in the most simple manner, as blessed Dr. Luther explained this article in a thoroughly Christian manner in a sermon at Torgau in 1533. He excluded all unprofitable and unnecessary questions, and exhorts all upright Christians to Christian simplicity of faith.

It is sufficient that we know that Christ descended into hell, that He destroyed hell for all believers, and that He delivered them from the power of death, the devil, and eternal damnation in the jaws of hell. How this was done we should save until the other world, [not research with curiosity, L.], when not only this article [mystery, L.], but others also will be revealed, which we could not comprehend here with our blind reason, but simply believed.

## X. CHURCH CUSTOMS
Which Are Called *Adiaphora,*
or Matters of Indifference

There has been controversy between the theologians of the Augsburg Confession also concerning ceremonies or church customs, which are neither commanded nor forbidden in God's Word, but have been introduced into the church for the sake of good order and decorum.

### The State of the Controversy
The Chief Dissension in This Article:

The main question has been, whether in a time of persecution and when the need for a confessional stand exists [*in casu confessionis,* L.], when the enemies of the Gospel are not in agreement with us in doctrine, whether one can then with a good conscience reintroduce discontinued ceremonies, even though they are in themselves matters of indifference, neither commanded nor forbidden by God, because the opponents urge and demand conformity with them in ceremonies and matters of indifference. The one side said yes, the other no.

### THE AFFIRMATIVE
The Right and True Doctrine and Confession Regarding This Article

1. To settle also this controversy, we unanimously believe, teach, and confess that the ceremonies or church customs which are neither commanded nor forbidden in God's Word, but are arranged only for for the sake of decorum and good order, are not *per se* and in themselves divine worship, nor any part of the same. Matt. 15:9; "In vain do they worship Me, teaching for doctrines the commandments of men."

2. We believe, teach, and confess that the congregation [*ecclesiae,* L.] of God of every time and place has authority according to the occasion [ *pro re nata,* L.] to change ceremonies, as it may be most useful and edifying to the congregation of God.

3. Yet that all levity and offense may be avoided in this matter, let the weak in faith be spared with all diligence. 1 Cor. 8:9-13; Rom. 14:1, 13 ff.

4. We believe, teach, and confess that at the time of persecution,

when a full [clear and constant, L.] confession is demanded of us, we should not yield to the enemies in indifferent matters. The apostles wrote: "Stand fast, therefore, in the liberty, wherewith Christ has made us free, and be not entangled again in the yoke of bondage," Gal. 5:1. Also: "Be ye not unequally yoked together with unbelievers. For what concord hath light with darkness?" 2 Cor. 6:14. Also, "To whom we gave place, no, not for an hour, that the truth of the Gospel might remain with you," Gal. 2:5. For in that case it is no longer a neutral matter, but concerns the truth of the Gospel, Christian liberty, the sanctioning of public idolatry, as also the prevention of offense to the weak in faith. In these matters we have nothing to concede, but should fully confess and on that account suffer what God sends us and allows the enemies of His Word to inflict upon us.

5. We believe, teach, and confess also that no church should condemn the other, because one has less or more ceremonies not commanded by God than the other, if there is unity in the doctrine and all its articles, as well as in the proper use of the holy sacraments according to the well-known saying: *Dissonantia jejunii non dissolvit consonantiam fidei.* Disagreement in fasting should not disrupt the agreement in faith (Irenaeus).

## THE NEGATIVE
False Doctrines Regarding This Article

Accordingly, we reject and condemn as false and contrary to the Word of God when it is taught:

1. That in the church the commandments of men may be accounted as divine worship in their own right, or a part of the same.

2. When such ceremonies, commandments, and rubrics are forced upon the church of God with duress, as though they were necessary, contrary to the Christian liberty which is ours in external matters.

3. Again, that in time of persecution, when a clear confession is required [L.], one may accede to the enemies of the Holy Gospel, though it serves to the detriment of the truth, and enter into agreement with them in matters neutral and ceremonial.

4. Also, when such external ceremonies and neutral matters are abrogated, as if the churches of God were not free to employ one or more of them in Christian liberty, as is most profitable at any given time or occasion.

## XI. GOD'S ETERNAL PREDESTINATION AND ELECTION

Regarding this article no public controversy broke out among the theologians of the Augsburg Confession. But since it is a comforting article when it is treated properly, it is explained in this document also, so that in the future no grievous disputation may be introduced.

## THE AFFIRMATIVE
The Pure, True Doctrine Concerning This Article

1. To begin with, the distinction between *praescientia* and *praedestinatione*, i.e., between the foreknowledge and the election by God, must be carefully observed.

2. For God's foreknowledge is nothing other than that He knows all things before they happen, as it is written: "There is a God in heaven that reveleath secrets and maketh known to the king Nebuchadnezzar what shall be in the latter days," Dan. 2:24 [KJV].

3. This foreknowledge extends equally to the good and to the evil, but it is not the cause of evil, nor of sins, as though men should thereby be impelled to sin. For sin comes originally from the devil and from the corrupted, evil will of man. Neither is the foreknowledge of God the cause of their destruction, for they are themselves to blame. The foreknowledge of God merely regulates the sin and sets its limits, how long it is to endure, and all this that it may serve the salvation of the elect, although it is evil in itself.

4. However, predestination or God's eternal election extends only over the godly, beloved children of God, and is a cause of their salvation. He it is who brings it about and determines all that belongs to it. Our salvation is so firmly founded upon it, that the "gates of hell" cannot overwhelm it, Matt. 16:18.

5. This predestination is not to be researched in the secret counsel of God, but is rather to be sought in the Word, in which it has been revealed.

6. Indeed, the Word leads to Christ, who is "the book of life" (Phil. 4:3; Rev. 3:5; 20:15), in whom all are recorded and elected who shall be eternally saved, as it is written: "He hath chosen us in Him (Christ) before the foundation of the world," Eph. 1:4.

7. This Christ calls all sinners to Himself and promises them new life. It is His earnest desire that all men should come to Him and allow themselves to be helped. He offers Himself to them in the Word and desires that they should hear and not stop their ears, nor despise the Word. In addition, He promises the power and working of the Holy Spirit, divine assistance for steadfastness, and eternal bliss.

8. For this reason we must not make a judgment regarding our election to eternal life according to our reason, nor according to the law of God, because these lead us either into a wild, uncontrolled Epicurean life, or into desperation, and arouse harmful thoughts in the hearts of men. They will be troubled in their mind and not be able to ward off such thoughts, as long as they follow their reason: If God has predestined me to salvation, then I cannot be damned, no matter

what I do; and vice versa: if I am not predestined to eternal life, the good that I do will be of no avail; it is all in vain.

9. On the contrary, it must be learned solely from Christ's holy Gospel, in which it is clearly attested, how "God hath concluded them all under unbelief, that He might have mercy upon all," (Rom. 11:32), and does not desire that anyone should perish, but that every man should repent and believe on the Lord Christ, Ezek. 33:11; 18:23; 1 Tim. 2:6.

10. Whoever is concerned about the revealed will of God and follows the order observed by St. Paul in the Epistle to the Romans, who first directs men to repentance, to acknowledgment of their sins, to faith in Christ, and to godly obedience before he speaks of the mystery of God's eternal election—to him this doctrine will be salutary [L.] and comforting.

11. It is not the meaning of the words, "Many are called, but few are chosen" (Matt. 20:16; 22:14), that God does not wish the salvation of all. The reason is rather that they either simply do not listen to God's Word, but wantonly despise it, harden their ears and their heart, thereby blocking the regular entrance for the Holy Ghost, so that He cannot perform His work in them—or, when they have heard it, they cast it to the winds again and do not heed it. God and His predestination cannot be held responsible for this, but their own malice.

12. A Christian should be receptive to the article of God's eternal election to the extent that it is revealed in God's Word, for it holds Christ before us as "the Book of Life." Through the preaching of the holy Gospel He unlocks this book for us and reveals to us, as is written: "Whom He did predestinate, them He also called," Rom. 8:30. In Him we should also seek the Father's election from eternity. In His eternal divine counsel He has decreed that, with the exception of those who acknowledge His Son, Christ, and truly believe in Him, He would grant salvation to none. Other thoughts should therefore be rejected, for they do not proceed from God, but from the inspiration of the evil foe, who boldly undertakes to weaken or even rob us of the heavenly comfort, which is ours through this salutary doctrine, namely, that we know that we have been predestined unto eternal life purely by grace in Christ, without any merit of ours, and that no man shall be able to pluck us out of His hand. Such a gracious election He not only promises in mere words, but confirms with an oath and seals with the holy sacraments, which we recall to our comfort in the deepest trials of faith, so that thereby we can quench the burning arrows of the devil.

13. At the same time we should expend every effort to live according to the will of God, and, as St. Peter admonishes, to "make our calling sure" (2 Peter 1:10), and, in particular, to hold fast to the revealed Word, which cannot and shall not fail us.

14. In this brief explanation of the eternal predestination by God complete and full honor is accorded to God, that He saves us according to the purpose of His will purely out of compassion, without any merit in us. On the contrary, no occasion is given to any man for either weakness of faith or for leading a coarse, abandoned life.

## THE NEGATIVE

False Doctrine on This Article

Accordingly we believe and hold that those who present the doctrine of God's gracious election unto eternal life in such a manner that troubled Christians cannot comfort themselves with it but are thrown into weakness of faith and into despair by it, or that the impenitent are strengthened in their wantonness, then this doctrine is not treated according to the Word and will of God, but according to reason and the prompting of a despicable Satan, because whatsoever was written, as the apostle testifies, was written for our instruction, "that we through patience and comfort of the Scriptures might have hope," Rom. 15:4. Therefore we reject the following errors:

1. When it is taught that God does not will that all mankind should repent and believe the Gospel.

2. Again, when God calls us to Him, that He does not seriously desire that all men should come to Him.

3. Again, that it is not God's will that everyone should be saved, but that regardless of their sin, some are destined unto damnation solely because of the bare decree, purpose, and will of God, so that they cannot be saved.

4. Again, that the mercy of God and the most holy merit of Christ are not solely the cause of God's election, but that a cause exists in us also, for which God predestined us unto eternal life.

All these are blasphemous and horrendous false teachings, by which Christians are deprived of all comfort which they have in the holy Gospel and in the use of holy sacraments. Therefore they should not be tolerated in the churches of God.

This is a short and simple explanation of the contested articles which for a time were disputed and taught by theologians of the Augsburg Confession in a controversial manner.

From this every simple Christian can observe under the guidance of God's Word and his simple *Catechism*, what is right or wrong. Not only the pure doctrine is stated, but the erring doctrine contrary to it is also set forth and rejected. Thus the offensive divisions that have erupted have been thoroughly adjudicated.

May the almighty God and Father of our Lord Jesus grant the grace of His Holy Spirit, that we may all be united in Him and remain constant in such Christian unity which is pleasing to Him. Amen.

# XII. OTHER HERESIES AND SECTS WHICH NEVER CONFESSED THE AUGSBURG CONFESSION

Lest they should be attributed to us, because we have not made mention of them in the preceding declaration, we have decided in the conclusion to make a bare listing of the articles in which errors are taught contrary to our Christian faith and confession, to which we have often referred.

## ERRONEOUS ARTICLES OF THE ANABAPTISTS

The Anabaptists are themselves divided into many groups, of which one group defends more, the other less error; in general, however, they promote a doctrine which can be tolerated or suffered neither by the church, nor by the civil and secular government, nor by the household.

### Articles Intolerable in the Church:

1. That Christ did not receive His body and blood from the Virgin Mary, but brought it with Him from heaven.
2. That Christ is not true God, but merely possesses more gifts of the Holy Spirit than any other sanctified person.
3. That our righteousness before God rests not only on the unique merit of Christ, but on our renewal and thus on our own piety and the life which we live. This is based largely on their own peculiar, self-chosen spirituality, and is, in fact, nothing but a new monasticism.
4. That unbaptized children are not sinners before God, but righteous and innocent, and that they will be saved in their innocence without Baptism (which they do not need according to this view), because they have not attained the use [L.] of their reason. Thus they reject the entire doctrine of original sin, and what pertains to it.
5. That children should not be baptized until they attain their reason and can themselves confess their faith.
6. That the children of Christians are holy, and are children of God even without and before Baptism, because they are born of Christian and believing parents. For this reason they do not regard the Baptism of children highly, and, contrary to the express word of promise, do not administer it. They hold that the promise extends only to those who keep God's covenant and do not despise it, Gen. 17:4-8, 19-21.
7. That no congregation in which sinners are still found can be truly Christian.
8. That one should not hear sermons, nor attend churches [*Tempel*, G.], in which papistic masses have previously been held and read.

9. That a pious [L.] man should have nothing to do with those ministers of the church, who preach according to the Augsburg Confession and condemn the preaching and the errors of the Anabaptists. One should do them no service nor work for them, but flee and avoid them as perverters of God's Word.

## Intolerable Articles Regarding Civil Government:

1. That civil government is not a God-pleasing estate in the New Testament.

2. That a Christian cannot with a good, inviolate conscience occupy nor administer an office of civil government.

3. That a Christian may not use the office of civil government in cases arising against criminals. Neither may he call upon its agents for protection and defense in line with their powers, which they have received from God.

4. That a Christian cannot with a good conscience swear an oath, nor do homage under oath to his hereditary landed prince or overlord.

5. That the civil government in the New Testament may not with a good conscience inflict capital punishment upon criminals.

## Intolerable Articles Regarding the Home:

1. That a Christian cannot with a good conscience keep nor possess private property, but that he is obligated to contribute it all [L.] to the commune.

2. That a Christian cannot with a good conscience be an innkeeper, a merchant, or a weaponsmith [*arma conficere*, L.].

3. That married people may be divorced on account of differing [L.] faith and forsake the other to marry another of his own faith.


# ERRING ARTICLES OF THE SCHWENKFELDIANS

1. That all those who regard Christ as a creature according to the flesh have no true understanding of Christ, the reigning King of heaven.

2. That Christ according to the flesh has by his exaltation taken to Himself all divine attributes in such a way, that Christ as a man is now essentially equal to the Father and the Word (Logos, John 1:1) in every degree and position, in might, power, majesty, and glory. There is now one essence, attribute, will, and glory of both natures in Christ, and that the flesh of Christ now belongs to the essence of the Holy Trinity.

3. That the ministry of the church—the preaching and hearing of the Word—is not a means, by which God the Holy Spirit teaches mankind and effects the saving knowledge of Christ, conversion, repentance, faith, and new obedience in them.

4. That the water of Baptism is not a means by which the Lord God seals the adoption of His children and effects their rebirth.

5. That bread and wine in Holy Communion are not means through which and with which Christ distributes His body and blood.

6. That a Christian person, truly reborn through the Holy Spirit, can keep and fulfill the law of God perfectly in this life.

7. There is no true Christian congregation where no public excommunication or orderly process of the ban is practiced.

8. That a minister of the church cannot profitably teach other people, nor rightly administer truly genuine sacraments, unless he is actually renewed, reborn, righteous, and pious in his own person.

## ERROR OF THE NEW ARIANS

That Christ is not truly, essentially, naturally God, of one eternal, divine essence with God the Father and the Holy Ghost, but merely adorned with divine majesty, inferior to and alongside of God the Father.

## ERROR OF THE ANTITRINITARIANS

This is an entirely new sect, not previously known in Christendom. They believe, teach, and confess, that there is not one unique, eternal, divine essence of the Father, Son, and Holy Ghost; but as God the Father, Son, and Holy Ghost are three distinct persons, so [they hold] each person has its own particular essence, distinct and separated from the other persons of the Godhead. Yet all three [some hold L.] are like three distinct people, separate from each other in essence, majesty, and glory, or [as others hold, L.] they are dissimilar in essence and attributes, so that the Father alone is true God.

These and all similar articles, and whatever further errors pertain to and proceed from them, we reject and condemn as wrong, false, heretical, and contrary to the Word of God, the three creeds, the Augsburg Confession, the Apology, the Smalcald Articles, and the Catechisms of Luther. All pious Christians of high or low estate should be on guard against them, as their soul's salvation and eternal bliss is dear to them.

That this is the teaching, faith, and confession of us all, for which we will give account on Judgment Day before the righteous Judge, our Lord Jesus Christ, and that we will not secretly or publicly speak or write anything against it, but by the grace of God intend to abide thereby, to this we have with forethought, in the fear of God, and calling upon His name, SUBSCRIBED WITH OUR HANDS.

Sealed: Berg, 29 May 1577

| | |
|---|---|
| Jacobus Andreae D. | Christophorus Cornerus D. |
| Nicolaus Selneccerus D. | David Chytraeus |
| Andreas Musculus D. | Martinus Kemnicius. D. |

# Questions

## GENERAL INTRODUCTION

*Topic question:*
What caused the troubled, divided condition of the Lutheran church after Luther's death?

Analytic questions:
1. What was remarkable about Luther's life? His death?
2. What resemblance is there between the Gospel and a passing shower?
3. In light of history, how does compromise of God's Word affect the church?
4. Who were some of the leading figures in the Smalcald War? How were the Lutherans affected by the resulting Augsburg Interim? Leipzig Interim?
5. Why was Melanchthon one of the most tragic figures of this era?
6. What was the role of Flacius?
7. How did the Lutherans manage to salvage their political life and existence?
8. Though the Peace of Augsburg (1555) gave the Lutherans a new status, why was peace in their own ranks still like a castle in the air?
9. Who were the leaders, and what was their contribution, in settling the sore divisions in the Lutheran church?

*Correlation:*
Spend some time with the opening statement or preface to the Epitome of the Formula of Concord, to catch the mood of the Confessors of 1577. What did they conceive their purpose to be in relation to the Augsburg Confession? Were they stating for their time, with a view toward the unsettling controversies, what in fact it meant to be a Lutheran in accord with the Augsburg Confession? Then discuss the pertinent relevance of this all for the church in our day. Is it perhaps possible—maybe even necessary eventually—that Lutherans who are concerned to be Lutherans according to the spirit and meaning of the Augsburg Confession, may have to express anew their stand over against false teachings that erode Scripture and Scriptural teaching in our time with a new document or confession?

*Conclusion:*
Discuss the significance of the old saying that if we do not learn from history we will have to repeat history's mistakes.

## EVENTS LEADING TO THE FORMULA OF CONCORD

*Topic question:*
How did the Formula of Concord and its Epitome come into being and succeed in healing the strife-torn Lutheran church?

Analytic questions:
1. In what way was the division in the Lutheran church after Luther's death similar to disputes in our day?
2. What lessons may be learned from lay and clergy involvement in the settlement of controversy?
3. Why is Crypto-Calvinism dangerous to Christianity?
4. If Chemnitz and Andreae were key personalities in resolving the deep cleavage, what factors in their lives and activities may be said to have been especially important?
5. What were the steps that led to the final formulation of the "Bergic Book" and the Epitome? What is important about the thesis and antithesis style instead of the sermonic? Was the guiding motive the writing of a new confession, or the spelling out of what it meant to stand for Confessional integrity?
6. Why was it better to circulate the documents for approval rather than to call for a church-wide assembly?
7. What principles should always underlie the church's efforts to achieve or maintain peace and unity?

*Correlation:*
Expand further, after reading this chapter, the pertinence of the prefatory remarks to the Epitome in our day. The *sola Scriptura* stand is particularly characteristic of the Lutheran church since the Reformation. Why is it significant that the Confessors were unequivocal in support of Scripture as the authoritative Word of God, and in acknowledging no other writings as "equal to the Holy Scriptures"? How is this attitude on Scripture's authority connected with their support of the ecumenical creeds, the Augsburg Confession and the Apology, Luther's Smalcald Articles, and the Catechisms, as faithful and correct expositions of Scriptural truth?

In view of the inroads of higher critical attacks on the Bible, where is the Word of God, if anywhere?

*Conclusion:*
Discuss the similarities between present-day controversies within the Lutheran church and those in the days prior to the "Bergic Book" and the Epitome; also the place of attitudes toward Scriptural authority.


I. ORIGINAL SIN

Topic questions:
Is original sin a part of man's being, or nature, as his body and soul are by creation? Or is it an intrusion, by and from the fall, into man's nature, radical and pervasive, but accidental nonetheless, that is not properly an essential part of man's being as man?

Analytic questions:
1. Who was Flacius and what role did he play in the Lutheran church after Luther?
2. What is the Flacian error? What is Manichaeism? Compare the two.
3. How do you explain that a man as competent as Flacius could have been snared by a trap like that set by Strigel?
4. In fending off synergism and man's capacity to aid in his conversion, how should one state the correct, Scriptural view of sin's impact on man?

5. Why must sin be described as *accidental* to man's nature and not *essential*?
6. Where did Luther stand on this matter? To what extent would he have agreed with Flacius? How would he have differed?
7. How did Strigel show his true colors?
8. Why does synergism, in every case, disavow the doctrine of man's total depravity?

*Correlation:*
Show the "Bergic Book's" or the Epitome's lucid rebuttal of the Flacian error, especially the implicit conflict between it and the rest of Christian teaching on creation, redemption, sanctification, glorification of man.

Explain, too, how Flacius's notion conflicted with Scripture's teaching concerning Christ's person.

Expand on the impressive list which the Epitome presents in summary of the faulty notions which have been held at various times concerning the evil in man's nature.

*Conclusion:*
The correct teaching concerning original sin has been described as the opposite side of the coin from the article on man's justification by God's grace alone through Christ by faith. Why is this an apt observation?


II. FREE WILL

Topic questions:
What part, if any, does the human will play in conversion or regeneration? Does Scripture's teaching on salvation *sola gratia*, by the grace of God alone, allow any room for man, or his will, as a contributing cause?

Analytic questions:
1. What is it that makes synergism such a persistent plague?
2. Why is Luther's encounter with Erasmus of such lasting significance?
3. Show that the Bible is not ambiguous on this question.
4. What difficulties are injected into the dispute because of human reason?
5. How shall one explain Melanchthon's tendencies in view of his close association with Luther?
6. Is Luther's position defensible on any other grounds save Scripture?
7. Does Luther deny man's inherent psychic equipment as a reality, as distinguishing man as man?
8. What part or role does the will of a regenerate person play in sanctification of life?
9. Where, then, lies the difference between Luther and Melanchthon?

*Correlation:*
The Epitome of the Formula speaks of "four dissimilar states" for the will of man. What significance does this have, and which state or condition is vital to our discussion?

The Epitome rules out the assenting will of man as a third factor in conversion. Which are the two that it recognizes?

Expand the Epitome's teaching concerning man's spiritual condition by nature and the need for the Holy Spirit's regenerating power.

List and explain the various erroneous teachings on this important article of faith.

*Conclusion:*
In speaking of God's drawing sinners to Himself in faith the Epitome highlights Scripture's teaching that conversion is solely *(solidum)* by God's grace and power, that by His grace He "makes willing men out of the obstreperously unwilling" (though not by coercion); and it (the Epitome) rejects the notion that "God draws, but He draws the willing." Explain why the proper distinction here is so vital.

### III. RIGHTEOUSNESS OF FAITH BEFORE GOD

Topic questions:
How is the believer righteous before God? By the grace of God gradually working the renewal of life and thus making his righteousness more complete? Or by God imputing to the believer the perfect righteousness which Christ won for all mankind?

Analytic questions:
1. What is meant by the statement that Christ is our righteousness?
2. What light does 2 Cor. 5:21 shed on the matter?
3. Why did Luther emphasize the difference between *declared*, or forensic, righteousness through Christ by faith, and being *made* righteous through Christ's indwelling of the believer by faith?
4. With which view would Rome be in agreement? Why? What would be involved if Osiander's view would have prevailed?
5. If the forensic sense of justification is upheld, why does this not exclude the power of Christ towards godliness in our lives?
6. What is the offense in "blood theology" to human reason and pride?
7. Is our justification complete and perfect through Christ, or must we first be made perfect for justification to be complete?
8. Granting that faith is not mere knowledge of stories about Jesus, how should its saving power be described?
9. How does the Formula of Concord distinguish between *regeneration* and *renewal* of life? Why?
10. Is Christ our righteousness according to one nature alone? If so, which? If not, why not?
11. Do both the active and passive obedience of Christ avail for our salvation? How may we distinguish them? Does *our* obedience also save?
12. How did the error of Stancarus differ from that of the Hamburg clergy?

*Correlation:*
The Epitome underscores the fact that Christ, true God and true man, achieved a perfect righteousness for us by perfectly fulfilling the Law and completely atoning for our guilt and punishment under the Law.

God's declaration of forgiveness because of Christ's atonement (forensic righteousness) is the ground of our salvation and the content of the Gospel proclamation.

In emphasizing faith-righteousness, or righteousness imputed unto faith, the Epitome seeks to uphold the great truth of forensic justification; at the same time it also recognizes the important effect that faith in Christ has on the believer's life for holiness and godly obedience; for regeneration will inevitably be followed by renewal of life.

The Epitome rightly rejected all teachings which detracted from the righteousness which is in and by Christ, as well as all teachings that detracted from His holy person and the personal union of natures in Him.

*Conclusion:*
This is the central article of the Christian faith. It is, therefore, not surprising that human reason and Satan should concentrate efforts here to confuse our understanding of what God has done for all sinners through Christ. Why has it been called the article on which the church stands or falls? Is that so for the individual Christian believer too?


## IV. GOOD WORKS

Topic question:
When we say that good works are a necessary part of every Christian's life, how is this to be understood?

Analytic questions:
1. What was the basic error in Major's and Melanchthon's thinking (and wording) on good works?
2. What is meant by "cheap grace"?
3. Why is it attractive to human nature to say that "good works are necessary to salvation"?
4. Do you think that it is useless dispute over words to distinguish between "necessary to salvation" and "necessary fruits of faith"? Explain.
5. How would you express Luther's position on the matter?
6. What happens to Christian certainty of salvation if Major's position stands?
7. Is it ever correct to say that good works are harmful to salvation? If so, when?
8. What was the antinomianism of Agricola? What was wrong with it? Why does a Christian need the guidance of God's Law in doing good works?
9. Does the believer have an obligation to do good works, according to the Epitome? Explain.


*Correlation:*
The dispute, as the Epitome showed, centered not only on the right understanding of the term "necessary" in connection with good works, but also on the proper place of God's Law in the Christian believer's life.
    The man who persists in his sinning and refuses to repent, hurts himself spiritually and may suffer eternal harm and make shipwreck of his faith.
    God rightly expects and is pleased by a godly life; but good works do not in themselves support or maintain faith; for faith is a work of the Holy Spirit alone. Good works are rightly spoken of as the necessary or inevitable fruit of faith, and they are a witness of the Holy Spirit's presence to the believer himself and to those around him.


*Conclusion:*
The Epitome shows that good works are a very real and very necessary part of a Christian believer's life. However, it is extremely important to see them in proper relationship to the righteousness which is ours by faith in Christ (Art. III). Growth in sanctification is God's will for His beloved; and such godliness is to be in accord with His holy Law, or will; but always as an *outgrowth* or fruit of faith in Christ, in whom we have full forgiveness and perfect righteousness before God.

## V. LAW AND GOSPEL

Topic questions:
What is the proper distinction between Law and Gospel? What is their proper sphere in a believer's life?

Analytic questions:
1. How can you determine whether a given verse or section of Scripture is Law or Gospel?
2. Why does hammer, rather than mirror, fit better Luther's explanation of the Law's principal, theological use?
3. Did the Law have the same function in the Old Testament as in the New, according to Luther? Why is this an important insight?
4. What was the antinomian teaching of Agricola?
5. If the Gospel is made to do what the Law is supposed to do, what happens to the Gospel?
6. Why does antinomianism become antigospelism?
7. Is it possible to preach the Gospel with power, if the Law's accusatory function has been eliminated?
8. Why is this important also in the life of the regenerate? (Compare what Paul says in Rom. 7.)
9. If the distinction between Law and Gospel goes, which other important distinctions are lost too?
10. What, if anything, is wrong with saying that the Law is the necessary form of the Gospel whose content is grace?

*Correlation:*
Christian preaching must include Law and Gospel, carefully measured out according to the needs of sinners, according to the Epitome.
 The distinction between Law and Gospel was not Luther's discovery or invention; it is the vital webbing of the whole fabric of God's Word.
 May some parts of Scripture, e.g., the suffering and death of Christ, also serve as a terrifying rebuke and proclamation of God's wrath against sin?
 Where is the Christian left, according to the Epitome, if the Gospel is transformed into a proclamation of legal demands and threats?

*Conclusion:*
Dr. C. F. W. Walther has put it well, drawing on Luther, who in turn drew on Paul's teaching (especially in Galatians), that the man who has the distinction between Law and Gospel uncluttered in his mind and heart, has the key to Scripture.


## VI. THIRD USE OF THE LAW

Topic question:
Does the Law continue to serve the regenerate believer as a guide or rule or standard of godly conduct?

Analytic questions:
1. When Luther said something like this: "The greatest knowledge in the world is not to know the Law," what did he mean?
2. Is it correct to divide the question this way: The Law in its political use, as

curb, is solely for the unregenerate, and in its theological use, as mirror or hammer, for the regenerate? Explain.
3. What did Agricola claim concerning the continuing need of the Law?
4. Why have some Lutherans then and now opposed the teaching that the Law still serves the Christian believer as teaching guide?
5. If "freedom in the Gospel" means that the man of faith no longer requires the guidance of God's Law, what will prevent people from opting for their own standards of conduct? What is situational ethics? Why would this be a threat to the individual Christian and the church?
6. Under what circumstances would teaching the third use of the Law make one a legalist, or an advocate of salvation by the Law?
7. Is "Gospelism," such as Agricola's, justified? Explain.
8. Did Luther teach the third use of the Law?
9. Why is the boast of the antinomians a threat to the Gospel?
10. In what, or where, does the power for godliness lie?

*Correlation:*
The Formula of Concord carefully delineated the threefold use of the Law. It also spoke about the Christian's freedom under the Law. Hence the two-pronged paradox: because the regenerate man is free from the Law's curse and penalty through Christ, he now delights in the very Law from which Christ has made him free.

The Epitome points out that the Law as curb is still necessary in the life of a Christian. Show how the Epitome distinguishes between "works of the Law" and "fruits of the Spirit," between the effect of God's Law in the penitent and the impenitent.

*Conclusion:*
God's Law continues to have a salutary use and function in the life of the regenerate man, in curbing his flesh, in working repentance, and in guiding his striving towards godliness.


VII. LORD'S SUPPER

Topic questions:
What does "Real Presence" mean? Do communicants (believing or unbelieving) receive the very body and blood which Christ says were given for them, or merely the bread and wine and a spiritualized presence of Christ?


Analytic questions:
1. Zwingli claimed that "is" in the words of institution meant "represents." Can "is" *ever* mean "represent?" When Christ says in figurative language, "I am the Door," does that mean He *represents* a door, or *is* He in fact the true Door, the only gateway, to the Father and everlasting life? Is the natural door the figure of Christ, the true Door, or vice versa?
2. Calvin said Jesus meant "this is my body symbolized." How did Luther counter this notion and prove it to be unscriptural?
3. What is the difference between trying to *explain* and *defining* the Lord's Supper and Christ's wonderful promise in the Sacrament?
4. What does every communicant (worthy or unworthy) receive in Holy Communion? Is it oral eating and drinking, or merely figurative?
5. Christ promises His personal presence to every believer in Matt. 28:20. Is this what He promises in the Lord's Supper? Why did He mention His body and blood, given for us, as His "new testament"? Does this mean

actually, really, substantively, though invisibly, or merely spiritually like His presence to faith? Is the manner of presence for His body and blood physical, like bread and wine, or is it in some nonphysical way, sacramentally, wondrously by His might and promise?

6. Is it any more difficult to believe that Christ is able to effect this wondrous promise of giving each communicant His body and blood wherever the Lord's Supper is properly celebrated, than to believe that He, the exalted Lord, is present everywhere according to the attribute of omnipresence which has also been communicated to His human nature through the incarnation?
7. Is it likely that those who deny Christ's Real Presence, His true body and blood in the Sacrament, will have a correct Scriptural teaching on the person and work of Christ?
8. What alone determines whether a guest at the Lord's Table is worthy or unworthy? What caution is in place concerning how we determine "worthiness"?
9. Ask yourself what properly belongs to a worthy celebration of the Lord's Supper? What not? What about peripheral customs, usages, ceremonies, etc.? Is there danger that Crypto-Calvinism, perhaps even Romanism, may creep into Lutheranism?

*Correlation:*
The Epitome carefully distinguished Lutheran teaching from the Romanist teaching of transubstantiation (and false adoration) and Reformed theology's symbolical presence of Christ (transignification). It showed, too, that the Lord's Supper properly is a sacrament, not a sacrifice.

We do not enhance the mystery of the Lord's Supper by "spiritualizing" or "mystifying" it by trying to make it a kind of "drama" reenacted.

The communion spoken of by the apostle in 1 Cor. 10:16 is clearly and first of all a communion of the elements—bread and body, wine and blood— and not of the communicants.

When Calvinists memorialize the "absent body and blood" of Christ, they are in fact limiting Christ's power of omnipresence.

No matter how well-intentioned, or pious, the teaching which spiritualizes the eating and drinking in the Sacrament contradicts Christ's clear and unambiguous promise.

Lutherans are neither Ubiquitists nor Capernaitic flesh eaters as they have been wrongly categorized by Calvinists.

The Epitome stressed that with the Lord's wondrous promise in Holy Communion "we have taken our reason captive" and that the mystery of the Lord's Supper is "comprehended solely by faith."

*Conclusion:*
Difference of opinion, of belief and teaching, on the Lord's Supper is serious. We either have the Lord's Supper as Christ instituted it, or we have another "supper" which is not the Lord's, no matter how earnest our intention. It is Christ's Word and promise which make the Sacrament, not our faith, or lack thereof.

VIII. PERSON OF CHRIST

Topic question:
Is there a true personal union, that is, a communion of natures (divine and human), and a communion of the attributes (divine and human) within Christ's person?

Analytic questions:
1. Why was it inevitable that confusion and false teaching concerning the Real Presence spin off with confusion on the person of Christ? Or, vice versa, why would erroneous views on Christ's person affect the teaching on the Lord's Supper?
2. Why did Melanchthon, who knew the article on Christ's person and work well, vacillate on the Lord's Supper?
3. What similarities are there between the controversies then and those that trouble the church now? Is the Gospel alone able to correct misguided notions? What alone can do that?
4. Why must the church at all times be concerned with pure doctrine?
5. Why is it important to emphasize the personal union of natures in Christ? Does each nature retain its essential properties? Does the person of Christ possess them all? Does Christ according to His human nature now share fully in the divine attributes, e.g., omnipotence, omnipresence? Why did our fathers compare this union of natures and communion of attributes to hot, fiery iron rather than two boards glued together?
6. Is Mary's son truly and fully the Son of God? and vice versa?
7. Would Christ have been able to suffer and die for us, if He had been the Son of God only and not also true man? On the other hand, would His holy Passion have been sufficient to atone for all mankind, if He had been true man only? Explain.
8. Luther based his teaching concerning the Real Presence of Christ's body and blood in the Sacrament on Christ's words of institution. But how did Scripture's teaching concerning the personal union of natures in Christ help him to understand, or be satisfied, with the wonder of what Christ here performed?
9. State and explain the errors that have appeared in the Christian church concerning the person of Christ.
10. How do errors concerning Christ's person and work threaten Christian faith?

*Correlation:*
The Epitome wove together in perfect harmony the articles on the Lord's Supper and the person of Christ. This is perhaps one of the most difficult and intricate sections in our Lutheran Confessions. Clarity and simplicity are of the essence.

The Epitome helps us to see that modern theology suffers from serious shortcomings because of confusion, shallowness, or false teaching on Christ's person and on other matters, e.g., the Lord's Supper.

There is no other recourse in this theological dilemma than the Reformation emphasis on *sola Scriptura/solo verbo,* by Scripture alone/by the Word alone.

*Conclusion:*
With cogent reason the Epitome reminds us and all readers that on this article concerning Christ's holy person and work, "if such false doctrine is not contradicted on the solid foundation of God's Word and our simple Christian creed, Christ will be lost altogether, along with our salvation."

God's doctrine is pure, and should be preserved that way, because it is given of God; in life there is sin and fault, because it is of men. If the latter is imperfect—and so often it is—it does not follow from this that doctrine may also be. In other words, while the church must be patient with sinners when they fall into sin and false beliefs, dare it be tolerant and patient with false teaching in the church?

## IX. DESCENT OF CHRIST INTO HELL

Topic questions:
What was the significance of Christ's descent into hell? Did it come as a climax of His suffering and humiliation, or was it the beginning of His exaltation and triumph?

Analytic questions:
1. Is the article on Christ's descent into hell important to faith? Could a person be saved, if he did not know it, or had faulty notions? What if he did know it but chose not to believe it?
2. If the Confessions teach it, is it necessary to have a Scriptural basis?
3. Do Lutherans believe something on Luther's authority? What significance does his testimony have?
4. Is it guesswork to say that Christ's descent was triumphant? That the whole person was involved?
5. Distinguish Aepinus's position from that of the scholastics and the Calvinistic, or Reformed, theologians.
6. Why did the Formula of Concord enter the fray, if Melanchthon was right in directing the disputants to Luther's Torgau sermon?

*Correlation:*
In speaking out clearly and firmly on this doctrine, which has relatively scant reference in the Bible, the Epitome demonstrated the principle of Lutheran theology that an article of faith is to be taught and believed even though Scripture refers to it but once, as long as that reference is clear and beyond cavil.

Knowing that the Confessions, especially the Apostles' Creed, may be very brief in their summation of Christian faith, what should this say to a Christian believer as he confesses the truth? What does he know and have as a result of Christ's descent into hell?

*Conclusion:*
When a Christian says that Christ conquered sin, death, and hell for him, these are very real, true, and important matters to him, both while he lives and when he dies. Christ's descent into hell is a keystone in Christian doctrine and in the Christian's faith and hope.

## X. CHURCH RITES

Topic questions:
May the church or the individual Christian compromise on adiaphora? Also in time of persecution, or when a confessional stand is required against the threat to Christian faith?

Analytic questions:
1. In what way is Melanchthon an object of sympathy?
2. Can we be sure that God will always have the last word, no matter how men plan and connive and politick? But what should be our stand under duress or persecution, or *in statu confessionis*?

3. What are adiaphora? Does this mean that a church should have random practices and no uniform usages or customs?
4. How do adiaphora differ from articles of faith?
5. Why does it sometimes become a matter of confession not to yield on matters which otherwise are free or open to choice? (Compare Gal. 2:3, 11-21; Jude 3.)
6. Why does Luther caution against making our liberty as Christians into a law? (Compare 1 Cor. 8 and 9; Rom. 14.)
7. What was the issue at the time of the Interims?
8. Were Melanchthon's Lutheran opponents right in opposing him?
9. What is unionism? What is the only right basis for churches that seek to establish fellowship?
10. What modern parallels and lessons suggest themselves from the adiaphoristic controversy of the 16th century?

*Correlation:*
The Epitome showed that when adiaphora are involved, the Christian individual and the Christian church must be careful not to coerce consciences, not to force uniformity or conformity.

However, what at one time, or under given circumstances, is free, or a matter of choice, may under duress and persecution become a confessional matter for the Christian believer who is being coerced to compromise his faith.

*Conclusion:*
The Christian conscience must be carefully respected not only in all matters of faith which are clearly taught in Scripture, but also in those things which God neither commands nor forbids. But conscience cannot claim immunity from taking a firm stand when certain rites and ceremonies, which otherwise are adiaphora, are demanded under duress. Then the Gospel itself may be under threat.


XI. GOD'S FOREKNOWLEDGE AND ELECTION

Topic questions:
Do all things happen as God foreknows them? Does this mean that He is the cause of evil things too? Does He elect those to salvation who He foresees will believe in Him? Or is God's election a distinct divine decree to which the believer, troubled by the onslaughts of Satan, the world, and his own flesh, looks with gratefulness and confidence, knowing that he who has God's promised forgiveness by faith in Christ also has God's assurance that he is numbered among the elect?

Analytic questions:
1. Does God foreknow all things? Are there accidents with God? (Compare 1 John 3:20; Ps. 139:1-18.)
2. Is God a mere spectator God over human activity and world events? Is there Scriptural ground for saying that He is responsible for sin and evil? Except for the prophets, on given occasion, is any man able to interpret God's ways and counsels? (Compare Rom. 11:33-36.)
3. May the believer in Christ look upon his faith as a wonderful fulfillment of God's eternal election? Or is he one of God's elect because God foresaw that he would cease from resisting and make his own decision for Christ? (Compare Rom. 8:28-39.)

4. How do the elect of God conduct themselves in life?(Compare Epitome XI, 13; 2 Peter 1:10.)
5. What is the error of synergism in the doctrine of election? What Scriptural teaching does it contradict?
6. What is the error of Calvinism? What Scriptural teaching does it contradict?
7. If a man is lost, who is responsible? If a man is saved, who is responsible?
8. How does the Formula of Concord solve the mystery of why some are saved, others lost?
9. List some mysteries connected with God's revelation of Himself and His purposes with which we go through life, content to know that God's revelation in Scripture is sufficient.
10. What parallel and lesson is there for the doctrinally divided church in Walther's handling of the predestinarian controversy?

*Correlation:*
The Epitome skilfully explains how confusion on God's foreknowledge and election inevitably involves false teaching on conversion, total depravity, free will, God's divine sovereignty, human accountability, etc.

The extremes of synergism and Calvinism need to be avoided. God is gracious unto all, not capricious or whimsical. But He will not be mocked; those who despise His grace through Christ will be damned.

Earnestly the Holy Spirit calls all to repentance and faith. His elect will hear His call and be saved.

*Conclusion:*
Ordinarily it is safest in theology to distinguish between divine foreknowledge and eternal election, as the Formula of Concord does. God's Word directs the sinner for his salvation to Christ, his Savior, in whom he has full and perfect redemption, and in whom he knows his election by God is sure.


XII. OTHER HERESIES AND SECTS

Topic questions:
What stand and action should the church take over against the sects? Against heretical and false teachings?

Analytic questions:
1. How did the Formula of Concord wish to distinguish what it said in Article XII from the preceding eleven articles?
2. Do the Scriptures and the Confessions have an injunction concerning orthodox teaching? What significance is there to Luther's distinction between doctrine and life, that doctrine must be pure because it is of God, while life is often marked with impurity, because it is in us?
3. Which were some of the sects troubling the 16th-century Lutheran church? What were their teachings? Should the church distinguish between those who deliberately, knowingly oppose God's truth, and those that do so in weakness or ignorance?
4. What were some of the common tendencies and false teachings running through the sects of that day? Are these still their characteristics?
5. What happens if the authority of the Word, Holy Scripture, is set aside or undermined? Is any basis for common consent left?

6. Since the Mennonites were less violent, is it also true that their theology was less objectionable?
7. Luther, and so Walther, always felt that where the essentials, or fundamentals, of Christian faith remained intact, there the Christian church could still be found. Would you agree with this? Does this constitute a sufficient basis for fellowship? What does this say concerning the Lutheran understanding of the doctrine of the church? Is the Lutheran church identical with the holy Christian church, the body of Christ? Are all Lutherans genuine Christians? What is a Christian? How do the Scriptures define the church? Should a person be concerned about being a member of an orthodox church, where Word and Sacraments are rightly and purely taught? (Compare AC VII and VIII) What is unionism? Why is it a sin? Why is it against Christian charity and love? What is the difference between tolerating sinners in the church and tolerating false teaching or false teachers in the church?
8. What is the difference between a cult and a sect?
9. Is Socinianism, or neo-Arianism, still a threat? Explain.

*Correlation:*
The Formula of Concord's concern with the sects and sectarian views always centered on the threat which they posed over against the fundamental articles of the Christian faith. Perversion of the Word of God led inevitably to false teachings in every direction, often also subverting the Gospel itself, also the natural orders, such as civil government, home, individual rights, liberty, property, and freedom of speech.

*Conclusion:*
Eternal vigilance is the price of freedom; undying respect for, love of, and belief in the Word of God is the bulwark of Christian faith and truth.

www.ingramcontent.com/pod-product-compliance
Lightning Source LLC
Chambersburg PA
CBHW020358170426
43200CB00005B/220